GW01045898

WINE NOTES

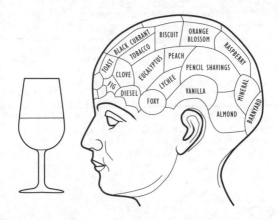

Wine is like music – it's nice in the background, but if you want to learn about it, a little focus is necessary.

WINE TASTING NOTEBOOK
By Steve De Long

THIRD EDITION

ISBN 978-1-936880-22-5
Printed in China

For more high quality winemaps, charts and books, visit
www.delongwine.com

 DE LONG

tasting date: location:

tasting partner(s):

wine name:

producer:

region/appellation:

grape varieties:

vintage: alcohol: price:

COLOR DEPTH:
watery | pale | medium | deep | dark

COLOR HUE:
WHITE: greenish | yellow | straw yellow | gold | amber
RED: purplish | ruby | red | garnet | brick | brown
ROSÉ: pink | salmon | orange | copper

CLARITY:
clear | slight haze | cloudy

AROMA INTENSITY:
low | moderate | aromatic | powerful

DEVELOPMENT:
youthful | some age | aged

AROMAS:

DRY/SWEET:
bone dry | dry | off dry | medium sweet | sweet | very sweet

BODY:
very light | light | medium | medium-full | full-bodied | heavy

ACIDITY:
tart | crisp | fresh | smooth | flabby

TANNINS (IF PRESENT):
LEVEL: low | medium | high   TYPE: soft | round | dry | hard

BALANCE:
good | fair | unbalanced (excess: alcohol - acid - tannin - sugar)

FLAVOR INTENSITY:
low | moderate | flavorful | powerful

FLAVORS:

FINISH:
short (< 3 sec) | medium (4-5) | long (5-7) | v. long (>8 sec)

CONCLUSION:

STYLE:
traditional | in-between | modern

rating: ☆ ☆ ☆ ☆ ☆

FOOD: **FOOD PAIRING:**

MATCH: perfect | good | neutral | bad

tasting date: location:

tasting partner(s):

wine name:

producer:

region/appellation:

grape varieties:

vintage: alcohol: price:

COLOR DEPTH:
watery | pale | medium | deep | dark

COLOR HUE:
WHITE: greenish | yellow | straw yellow | gold | amber
RED: purplish | ruby | red | garnet | brick | brown
ROSÉ: pink | salmon | orange | copper

CLARITY:
clear | slight haze | cloudy

AROMA INTENSITY:
low | moderate | aromatic | powerful

DEVELOPMENT:
youthful | some age | aged

AROMAS:

DRY/SWEET:
bone dry | dry | off dry | medium sweet | sweet | very sweet

BODY:
very light | light | medium | medium-full | full-bodied | heavy

ACIDITY:
tart | crisp | fresh | smooth | flabby

TANNINS (IF PRESENT):
LEVEL: low | medium | high   TYPE: soft | round | dry | hard

BALANCE:
good | fair | unbalanced (excess: alcohol - acid - tannin - sugar)

FLAVOR INTENSITY:
low | moderate | flavorful | powerful

FLAVORS:

FINISH:
short (< 3 sec) | medium (4-5) | long (5-7) | v. long (>8 sec)

CONCLUSION:

STYLE:
traditional | in-between | modern

rating: ☆ ☆ ☆ ☆ ☆

FOOD: **FOOD PAIRING:**

MATCH: perfect | good | neutral | bad

tasting date: location:

tasting partner(s):

wine name:

producer:

region/appellation:

grape varieties:

vintage: alcohol: price:

COLOR DEPTH:
watery | pale | medium | deep | dark

COLOR HUE:
WHITE: greenish | yellow | straw yellow | gold | amber
RED: purplish | ruby | red | garnet | brick | brown
ROSÉ: pink | salmon | orange | copper

CLARITY:
clear | slight haze | cloudy

AROMA INTENSITY:
low | moderate | aromatic | powerful

DEVELOPMENT:
youthful | some age | aged

AROMAS:

DRY/SWEET:
bone dry | dry | off dry | medium sweet | sweet | very sweet

BODY:
very light | light | medium | medium-full | full-bodied | heavy

ACIDITY:
tart | crisp | fresh | smooth | flabby

TANNINS (IF PRESENT):
LEVEL: low | medium | high   TYPE: soft | round | dry | hard

BALANCE:
good | fair | unbalanced (excess: alcohol - acid - tannin - sugar)

FLAVOR INTENSITY:
low | moderate | flavorful | powerful

FLAVORS:

FINISH:
short (< 3 sec) | medium (4-5) | long (5-7) | v. long (>8 sec)

CONCLUSION:

STYLE:
traditional | in-between | modern

rating: ☆ ☆ ☆ ☆ ☆

FOOD: **FOOD PAIRING:**

MATCH: perfect | good | neutral | bad

tasting date: location:

tasting partner(s):

wine name:

producer:

region/appellation:

grape varieties:

vintage: alcohol: price:

COLOR DEPTH:
watery | pale | medium | deep | dark

COLOR HUE:
WHITE: greenish | yellow | straw yellow | gold | amber
RED: purplish | ruby | red | garnet | brick | brown
ROSÉ: pink | salmon | orange | copper

CLARITY:
clear | slight haze | cloudy

AROMA INTENSITY:
low | moderate | aromatic | powerful

DEVELOPMENT:
youthful | some age | aged

AROMAS:

DRY/SWEET:
bone dry | dry | off dry | medium sweet | sweet | very sweet

BODY:
very light | light | medium | medium-full | full-bodied | heavy

ACIDITY:
tart | crisp | fresh | smooth | flabby

TANNINS (IF PRESENT):
LEVEL: low | medium | high   TYPE: soft | round | dry | hard

BALANCE:
good | fair | unbalanced (excess: alcohol - acid - tannin - sugar)

FLAVOR INTENSITY:
low | moderate | flavorful | powerful

FLAVORS:

FINISH:
short (< 3 sec) | medium (4-5) | long (5-7) | v. long (>8 sec)

CONCLUSION:

STYLE:
traditional | in-between | modern

rating: ☆ ☆ ☆ ☆ ☆

FOOD: **FOOD PAIRING:**

MATCH: perfect | good | neutral | bad

tasting date: location:

tasting partner(s):

wine name:

producer:

region/appellation:

grape varieties:

vintage: alcohol: price:

COLOR DEPTH:
watery | pale | medium | deep | dark

COLOR HUE:
WHITE: greenish | yellow | straw yellow | gold | amber
RED: purplish | ruby | red | garnet | brick | brown
ROSÉ: pink | salmon | orange | copper

CLARITY:
clear | slight haze | cloudy

AROMA INTENSITY:
low | moderate | aromatic | powerful

DEVELOPMENT:
youthful | some age | aged

AROMAS:

DRY/SWEET:
bone dry | dry | off dry | medium sweet | sweet | very sweet

BODY:
very light | light | medium | medium-full | full-bodied | heavy

ACIDITY:
tart | crisp | fresh | smooth | flabby

TANNINS (IF PRESENT):
LEVEL: low | medium | high   TYPE: soft | round | dry | hard

BALANCE:
good | fair | unbalanced (excess: alcohol - acid - tannin - sugar)

FLAVOR INTENSITY:
low | moderate | flavorful | powerful

FLAVORS:

FINISH:
short (< 3 sec) | medium (4-5) | long (5-7) | v. long (>8 sec)

CONCLUSION:

STYLE:
traditional | in-between | modern

rating: ☆ ☆ ☆ ☆ ☆

FOOD: **FOOD PAIRING:**
MATCH: perfect | good | neutral | bad

tasting date: location:

tasting partner(s):

wine name:

producer:

region/appellation:

grape varieties:

vintage: alcohol: price:

COLOR DEPTH:
watery | pale | medium | deep | dark

COLOR HUE:
WHITE: greenish | yellow | straw yellow | gold | amber
RED: purplish | ruby | red | garnet | brick | brown
ROSÉ: pink | salmon | orange | copper

CLARITY:
clear | slight haze | cloudy

AROMA INTENSITY:
low | moderate | aromatic | powerful

DEVELOPMENT:
youthful | some age | aged

AROMAS:

DRY/SWEET:
bone dry | dry | off dry | medium sweet | sweet | very sweet

BODY:
very light | light | medium | medium-full | full-bodied | heavy

ACIDITY:
tart | crisp | fresh | smooth | flabby

TANNINS (IF PRESENT):
LEVEL: low | medium | high   TYPE: soft | round | dry | hard

BALANCE:
good | fair | unbalanced (excess: alcohol - acid - tannin - sugar)

FLAVOR INTENSITY:
low | moderate | flavorful | powerful

FLAVORS:

FINISH:
short (< 3 sec) | medium (4-5) | long (5-7) | v. long (>8 sec)

CONCLUSION:

STYLE:
traditional | in-between | modern

rating: ☆ ☆ ☆ ☆ ☆

FOOD: **FOOD PAIRING:**

                 MATCH: perfect | good | neutral | bad

tasting date: location:

tasting partner(s):

wine name:

producer:

region/appellation:

grape varieties:

vintage: alcohol: price:

COLOR DEPTH:
watery | pale | medium | deep | dark

COLOR HUE:
WHITE: greenish | yellow | straw yellow | gold | amber
RED: purplish | ruby | red | garnet | brick | brown
ROSÉ: pink | salmon | orange | copper

CLARITY:
clear | slight haze | cloudy

AROMA INTENSITY:
low | moderate | aromatic | powerful

DEVELOPMENT:
youthful | some age | aged

AROMAS:

DRY/SWEET:
bone dry | dry | off dry | medium sweet | sweet | very sweet

BODY:
very light | light | medium | medium-full | full-bodied | heavy

ACIDITY:
tart | crisp | fresh | smooth | flabby

TANNINS (IF PRESENT):
LEVEL: low | medium | high   TYPE: soft | round | dry | hard

BALANCE:
good | fair | unbalanced (excess: alcohol - acid - tannin - sugar)

FLAVOR INTENSITY:
low | moderate | flavorful | powerful

FLAVORS:

FINISH:
short (< 3 sec) | medium (4-5) | long (5-7) | v. long (>8 sec)

CONCLUSION:

STYLE:
traditional | in-between | modern

rating: ☆ ☆ ☆ ☆ ☆

FOOD: **FOOD PAIRING:**

MATCH: perfect | good | neutral | bad

tasting date: location:

tasting partner(s):

wine name:

producer:

region/appellation:

grape varieties:

vintage: alcohol: price:

COLOR DEPTH:
watery | pale | medium | deep | dark

COLOR HUE:
WHITE: greenish | yellow | straw yellow | gold | amber
RED: purplish | ruby | red | garnet | brick | brown
ROSÉ: pink | salmon | orange | copper

CLARITY:
clear | slight haze | cloudy

AROMA INTENSITY:
low | moderate | aromatic | powerful

DEVELOPMENT:
youthful | some age | aged

AROMAS:

DRY/SWEET:
bone dry | dry | off dry | medium sweet | sweet | very sweet

BODY:
very light | light | medium | medium-full | full-bodied | heavy

ACIDITY:
tart | crisp | fresh | smooth | flabby

TANNINS (IF PRESENT):
LEVEL: low | medium | high   TYPE: soft | round | dry | hard

BALANCE:
good | fair | unbalanced (excess: alcohol - acid - tannin - sugar)

FLAVOR INTENSITY:
low | moderate | flavorful | powerful

FLAVORS:

FINISH:
short (< 3 sec) | medium (4-5) | long (5-7) | v. long (>8 sec)

CONCLUSION:

STYLE:
traditional | in-between | modern

rating: ☆ ☆ ☆ ☆ ☆

FOOD: **FOOD PAIRING:**
              MATCH: perfect | good | neutral | bad

tasting date: location:

tasting partner(s):

wine name:

producer:

region/appellation:

grape varieties:

vintage: alcohol: price:

COLOR DEPTH:
watery | pale | medium | deep | dark

COLOR HUE:
WHITE: greenish | yellow | straw yellow | gold | amber
RED: purplish | ruby | red | garnet | brick | brown
ROSÉ: pink | salmon | orange | copper

CLARITY:
clear | slight haze | cloudy

AROMA INTENSITY:
low | moderate | aromatic | powerful

DEVELOPMENT:
youthful | some age | aged

AROMAS:

DRY/SWEET:
bone dry | dry | off dry | medium sweet | sweet | very sweet

BODY:
very light | light | medium | medium-full | full-bodied | heavy

ACIDITY:
tart | crisp | fresh | smooth | flabby

TANNINS (IF PRESENT):
LEVEL: low | medium | high   TYPE: soft | round | dry | hard

BALANCE:
good | fair | unbalanced (excess: alcohol - acid - tannin - sugar)

FLAVOR INTENSITY:
low | moderate | flavorful | powerful

FLAVORS:

FINISH:
short (< 3 sec) | medium (4-5) | long (5-7) | v. long (>8 sec)

CONCLUSION:

STYLE:
traditional | in-between | modern

rating: ☆ ☆ ☆ ☆ ☆

FOOD: **FOOD PAIRING:**
                 MATCH: perfect | good | neutral | bad

tasting date: location:

tasting partner(s):

wine name:

producer:

region/appellation:

grape varieties:

vintage: alcohol: price:

COLOR DEPTH:
watery | pale | medium | deep | dark

COLOR HUE:
WHITE: greenish | yellow | straw yellow | gold | amber
RED: purplish | ruby | red | garnet | brick | brown
ROSÉ: pink | salmon | orange | copper

CLARITY:
clear | slight haze | cloudy

AROMA INTENSITY:
low | moderate | aromatic | powerful

DEVELOPMENT:
youthful | some age | aged

AROMAS:

DRY/SWEET:
bone dry | dry | off dry | medium sweet | sweet | very sweet

BODY:
very light | light | medium | medium-full | full-bodied | heavy

ACIDITY:
tart | crisp | fresh | smooth | flabby

TANNINS (IF PRESENT):
LEVEL: low | medium | high   TYPE: soft | round | dry | hard

BALANCE:
good | fair | unbalanced (excess: alcohol - acid - tannin - sugar)

FLAVOR INTENSITY:
low | moderate | flavorful | powerful

FLAVORS:

FINISH:
short (< 3 sec) | medium (4-5) | long (5-7) | v. long (>8 sec)

CONCLUSION:

STYLE:
traditional | in-between | modern

rating: ☆ ☆ ☆ ☆ ☆

FOOD: ## FOOD PAIRING:
            MATCH: perfect | good | neutral | bad

tasting date: location:

tasting partner(s):

wine name:

producer:

region/appellation:

grape varieties:

vintage: alcohol: price:

COLOR DEPTH:
watery | pale | medium | deep | dark
COLOR HUE:
WHITE: greenish | yellow | straw yellow | gold | amber
RED: purplish | ruby | red | garnet | brick | brown
ROSÉ: pink | salmon | orange | copper

CLARITY:
clear | slight haze | cloudy

AROMA INTENSITY:
low | moderate | aromatic | powerful
DEVELOPMENT:
youthful | some age | aged
AROMAS:

DRY/SWEET:
bone dry | dry | off dry | medium sweet | sweet | very sweet
BODY:
very light | light | medium | medium-full | full-bodied | heavy
ACIDITY:
tart | crisp | fresh | smooth | flabby
TANNINS (IF PRESENT):
LEVEL: low | medium | high   TYPE: soft | round | dry | hard
BALANCE:
good | fair | unbalanced (excess: alcohol - acid - tannin - sugar)
FLAVOR INTENSITY:
low | moderate | flavorful | powerful
FLAVORS:

FINISH:
short (< 3 sec) | medium (4-5) | long (5-7) | v. long (>8 sec)

CONCLUSION:

STYLE:
traditional | in-between | modern

rating: ☆ ☆ ☆ ☆ ☆

FOOD: **FOOD PAIRING:**
MATCH: perfect | good | neutral | bad

tasting date: location:

tasting partner(s):

wine name:

producer:

region/appellation:

grape varieties:

vintage: alcohol: price:

COLOR DEPTH:
watery | pale | medium | deep | dark

COLOR HUE:
WHITE: greenish | yellow | straw yellow | gold | amber
RED: purplish | ruby | red | garnet | brick | brown
ROSÉ: pink | salmon | orange | copper

CLARITY:
clear | slight haze | cloudy

AROMA INTENSITY:
low | moderate | aromatic | powerful

DEVELOPMENT:
youthful | some age | aged

AROMAS:

DRY/SWEET:
bone dry | dry | off dry | medium sweet | sweet | very sweet

BODY:
very light | light | medium | medium-full | full-bodied | heavy

ACIDITY:
tart | crisp | fresh | smooth | flabby

TANNINS (IF PRESENT):
LEVEL: low | medium | high   TYPE: soft | round | dry | hard

BALANCE:
good | fair | unbalanced (excess: alcohol - acid - tannin - sugar)

FLAVOR INTENSITY:
low | moderate | flavorful | powerful

FLAVORS:

FINISH:
short (< 3 sec) | medium (4-5) | long (5-7) | v. long (>8 sec)

CONCLUSION:

STYLE:
traditional | in-between | modern

rating: ☆ ☆ ☆ ☆ ☆

FOOD: **FOOD PAIRING:**

MATCH: perfect | good | neutral | bad

tasting date: location:

tasting partner(s):

wine name:

producer:

region/appellation:

grape varieties:

vintage: alcohol: price:

COLOR DEPTH:
watery | pale | medium | deep | dark

COLOR HUE:
WHITE: greenish | yellow | straw yellow | gold | amber
RED: purplish | ruby | red | garnet | brick | brown
ROSÉ: pink | salmon | orange | copper

CLARITY:
clear | slight haze | cloudy

AROMA INTENSITY:
low | moderate | aromatic | powerful

DEVELOPMENT:
youthful | some age | aged

AROMAS:

DRY/SWEET:
bone dry | dry | off dry | medium sweet | sweet | very sweet

BODY:
very light | light | medium | medium-full | full-bodied | heavy

ACIDITY:
tart | crisp | fresh | smooth | flabby

TANNINS (IF PRESENT):
LEVEL: low | medium | high   TYPE: soft | round | dry | hard

BALANCE:
good | fair | unbalanced (excess: alcohol - acid - tannin - sugar)

FLAVOR INTENSITY:
low | moderate | flavorful | powerful

FLAVORS:

FINISH:
short (< 3 sec) | medium (4-5) | long (5-7) | v. long (>8 sec)

CONCLUSION:

STYLE:
traditional | in-between | modern

rating: ☆ ☆ ☆ ☆ ☆

FOOD: **FOOD PAIRING:**

MATCH: perfect | good | neutral | bad

tasting date: location:

tasting partner(s):

wine name:

producer:

region/appellation:

grape varieties:

vintage: alcohol: price:

COLOR DEPTH:
watery | pale | medium | deep | dark

COLOR HUE:
WHITE: greenish | yellow | straw yellow | gold | amber
RED: purplish | ruby | red | garnet | brick | brown
ROSÉ: pink | salmon | orange | copper

CLARITY:
clear | slight haze | cloudy

AROMA INTENSITY:
low | moderate | aromatic | powerful

DEVELOPMENT:
youthful | some age | aged

AROMAS:

DRY/SWEET:
bone dry | dry | off dry | medium sweet | sweet | very sweet

BODY:
very light | light | medium | medium-full | full-bodied | heavy

ACIDITY:
tart | crisp | fresh | smooth | flabby

TANNINS (IF PRESENT):
LEVEL: low | medium | high   TYPE: soft | round | dry | hard

BALANCE:
good | fair | unbalanced (excess: alcohol - acid - tannin - sugar)

FLAVOR INTENSITY:
low | moderate | flavorful | powerful

FLAVORS:

FINISH:
short (< 3 sec) | medium (4-5) | long (5-7) | v. long (>8 sec)

CONCLUSION:

STYLE:
traditional | in-between | modern

rating: ☆ ☆ ☆ ☆ ☆

FOOD: **FOOD PAIRING:**

MATCH: perfect | good | neutral | bad

tasting date: location:

tasting partner(s):

wine name:

producer:

region/appellation:

grape varieties:

vintage: alcohol: price:

COLOR DEPTH:
watery | pale | medium | deep | dark

COLOR HUE:
WHITE: greenish | yellow | straw yellow | gold | amber
RED: purplish | ruby | red | garnet | brick | brown
ROSÉ: pink | salmon | orange | copper

CLARITY:
clear | slight haze | cloudy

AROMA INTENSITY:
low | moderate | aromatic | powerful

DEVELOPMENT:
youthful | some age | aged

AROMAS:

DRY/SWEET:
bone dry | dry | off dry | medium sweet | sweet | very sweet

BODY:
very light | light | medium | medium-full | full-bodied | heavy

ACIDITY:
tart | crisp | fresh | smooth | flabby

TANNINS (IF PRESENT):
LEVEL: low | medium | high   TYPE: soft | round | dry | hard

BALANCE:
good | fair | unbalanced (excess: alcohol - acid - tannin - sugar)

FLAVOR INTENSITY:
low | moderate | flavorful | powerful

FLAVORS:

FINISH:
short (< 3 sec) | medium (4-5) | long (5-7) | v. long (>8 sec)

CONCLUSION:

STYLE:
traditional | in-between | modern

rating: ☆ ☆ ☆ ☆ ☆

FOOD: ### FOOD PAIRING:
MATCH: perfect | good | neutral | bad

tasting date: location:

tasting partner(s):

wine name:

producer:

region/appellation:

grape varieties:

vintage: alcohol: price:

COLOR DEPTH:
watery | pale | medium | deep | dark

COLOR HUE:
WHITE: greenish | yellow | straw yellow | gold | amber
RED: purplish | ruby | red | garnet | brick | brown
ROSÉ: pink | salmon | orange | copper

CLARITY:
clear | slight haze | cloudy

AROMA INTENSITY:
low | moderate | aromatic | powerful

DEVELOPMENT:
youthful | some age | aged

AROMAS:

DRY/SWEET:
bone dry | dry | off dry | medium sweet | sweet | very sweet

BODY:
very light | light | medium | medium-full | full-bodied | heavy

ACIDITY:
tart | crisp | fresh | smooth | flabby

TANNINS (IF PRESENT):
LEVEL: low | medium | high   TYPE: soft | round | dry | hard

BALANCE:
good | fair | unbalanced (excess: alcohol - acid - tannin - sugar)

FLAVOR INTENSITY:
low | moderate | flavorful | powerful

FLAVORS:

FINISH:
short (< 3 sec) | medium (4-5) | long (5-7) | v. long (>8 sec)

CONCLUSION:

STYLE:
traditional | in-between | modern

rating: ☆ ☆ ☆ ☆ ☆

FOOD: **FOOD PAIRING:**

MATCH: perfect | good | neutral | bad

tasting date: location:

tasting partner(s):

wine name:

producer:

region/appellation:

grape varieties:

vintage: alcohol: price:

COLOR DEPTH:
watery | pale | medium | deep | dark

COLOR HUE:
WHITE: greenish | yellow | straw yellow | gold | amber
RED: purplish | ruby | red | garnet | brick | brown
ROSÉ: pink | salmon | orange | copper

CLARITY:
clear | slight haze | cloudy

AROMA INTENSITY:
low | moderate | aromatic | powerful

DEVELOPMENT:
youthful | some age | aged

AROMAS:

DRY/SWEET:
bone dry | dry | off dry | medium sweet | sweet | very sweet

BODY:
very light | light | medium | medium-full | full-bodied | heavy

ACIDITY:
tart | crisp | fresh | smooth | flabby

TANNINS (IF PRESENT):
LEVEL: low | medium | high   TYPE: soft | round | dry | hard

BALANCE:
good | fair | unbalanced (excess: alcohol - acid - tannin - sugar)

FLAVOR INTENSITY:
low | moderate | flavorful | powerful

FLAVORS:

FINISH:
short (< 3 sec) | medium (4-5) | long (5-7) | v. long (>8 sec)

CONCLUSION:

STYLE:
traditional | in-between | modern

rating: ☆ ☆ ☆ ☆ ☆

FOOD: **FOOD PAIRING:**
MATCH: perfect | good | neutral | bad

tasting date: location:

tasting partner(s):

wine name:

producer:

region/appellation:

grape varieties:

vintage: alcohol: price:

COLOR DEPTH:
watery | pale | medium | deep | dark

COLOR HUE:
WHITE: greenish | yellow | straw yellow | gold | amber
RED: purplish | ruby | red | garnet | brick | brown
ROSÉ: pink | salmon | orange | copper

CLARITY:
clear | slight haze | cloudy

AROMA INTENSITY:
low | moderate | aromatic | powerful

DEVELOPMENT:
youthful | some age | aged

AROMAS:

DRY/SWEET:
bone dry | dry | off dry | medium sweet | sweet | very sweet

BODY:
very light | light | medium | medium-full | full-bodied | heavy

ACIDITY:
tart | crisp | fresh | smooth | flabby

TANNINS (IF PRESENT):
LEVEL: low | medium | high   TYPE: soft | round | dry | hard

BALANCE:
good | fair | unbalanced (excess: alcohol - acid - tannin - sugar)

FLAVOR INTENSITY:
low | moderate | flavorful | powerful

FLAVORS:

FINISH:
short (< 3 sec) | medium (4-5) | long (5-7) | v. long (>8 sec)

CONCLUSION:

STYLE:
traditional | in-between | modern

rating: ☆ ☆ ☆ ☆ ☆

FOOD: **FOOD PAIRING:**

MATCH: perfect | good | neutral | bad

tasting date: location:

tasting partner(s):

wine name:

producer:

region/appellation:

grape varieties:

vintage: alcohol: price:

COLOR DEPTH:
watery | pale | medium | deep | dark

COLOR HUE:
WHITE: greenish | yellow | straw yellow | gold | amber
RED: purplish | ruby | red | garnet | brick | brown
ROSÉ: pink | salmon | orange | copper

CLARITY:
clear | slight haze | cloudy

AROMA INTENSITY:
low | moderate | aromatic | powerful

DEVELOPMENT:
youthful | some age | aged

AROMAS:

DRY/SWEET:
bone dry | dry | off dry | medium sweet | sweet | very sweet

BODY:
very light | light | medium | medium-full | full-bodied | heavy

ACIDITY:
tart | crisp | fresh | smooth | flabby

TANNINS (IF PRESENT):
LEVEL: low | medium | high   TYPE: soft | round | dry | hard

BALANCE:
good | fair | unbalanced (excess: alcohol - acid - tannin - sugar)

FLAVOR INTENSITY:
low | moderate | flavorful | powerful

FLAVORS:

FINISH:
short (< 3 sec) | medium (4-5) | long (5-7) | v. long (>8 sec)

CONCLUSION:

STYLE:
traditional | in-between | modern

rating: ☆ ☆ ☆ ☆ ☆

FOOD: **FOOD PAIRING:**

MATCH: perfect | good | neutral | bad

tasting date: location:

tasting partner(s):

wine name:

producer:

region/appellation:

grape varieties:

vintage: alcohol: price:

COLOR DEPTH:
watery | pale | medium | deep | dark

COLOR HUE:
WHITE: greenish | yellow | straw yellow | gold | amber
RED: purplish | ruby | red | garnet | brick | brown
ROSÉ: pink | salmon | orange | copper

CLARITY:
clear | slight haze | cloudy

AROMA INTENSITY:
low | moderate | aromatic | powerful

DEVELOPMENT:
youthful | some age | aged

AROMAS:

DRY/SWEET:
bone dry | dry | off dry | medium sweet | sweet | very sweet

BODY:
very light | light | medium | medium-full | full-bodied | heavy

ACIDITY:
tart | crisp | fresh | smooth | flabby

TANNINS (IF PRESENT):
LEVEL: low | medium | high   TYPE: soft | round | dry | hard

BALANCE:
good | fair | unbalanced (excess: alcohol - acid - tannin - sugar)

FLAVOR INTENSITY:
low | moderate | flavorful | powerful

FLAVORS:

FINISH:
short (< 3 sec) | medium (4-5) | long (5-7) | v. long (>8 sec)

CONCLUSION:

STYLE:
traditional | in-between | modern

rating: ☆☆☆☆☆

FOOD: ## FOOD PAIRING:

MATCH: perfect | good | neutral | bad

tasting date: location:

tasting partner(s):

wine name:

producer:

region/appellation:

grape varieties:

vintage: alcohol: price:

COLOR DEPTH:
watery | pale | medium | deep | dark
COLOR HUE:
WHITE: greenish | yellow | straw yellow | gold | amber
RED: purplish | ruby | red | garnet | brick | brown
ROSÉ: pink | salmon | orange | copper
CLARITY:
clear | slight haze | cloudy

AROMA INTENSITY:
low | moderate | aromatic | powerful
DEVELOPMENT:
youthful | some age | aged
AROMAS:

DRY/SWEET:
bone dry | dry | off dry | medium sweet | sweet | very sweet
BODY:
very light | light | medium | medium-full | full-bodied | heavy
ACIDITY:
tart | crisp | fresh | smooth | flabby
TANNINS (IF PRESENT):
LEVEL: low | medium | high   TYPE: soft | round | dry | hard
BALANCE:
good | fair | unbalanced (excess: alcohol - acid - tannin - sugar)
FLAVOR INTENSITY:
low | moderate | flavorful | powerful
FLAVORS:

FINISH:
short (< 3 sec) | medium (4-5) | long (5-7) | v. long (>8 sec)
CONCLUSION:

STYLE:
traditional | in-between | modern
rating: ☆ ☆ ☆ ☆ ☆

FOOD: **FOOD PAIRING:**
                  MATCH: perfect | good | neutral | bad

tasting date: location:

tasting partner(s):

wine name:

producer:

region/appellation:

grape varieties:

vintage: alcohol: price:

COLOR DEPTH:
watery | pale | medium | deep | dark

COLOR HUE:
WHITE: greenish | yellow | straw yellow | gold | amber
RED: purplish | ruby | red | garnet | brick | brown
ROSÉ: pink | salmon | orange | copper

CLARITY:
clear | slight haze | cloudy

AROMA INTENSITY:
low | moderate | aromatic | powerful

DEVELOPMENT:
youthful | some age | aged

AROMAS:

DRY/SWEET:
bone dry | dry | off dry | medium sweet | sweet | very sweet

BODY:
very light | light | medium | medium-full | full-bodied | heavy

ACIDITY:
tart | crisp | fresh | smooth | flabby

TANNINS (IF PRESENT):
LEVEL: low | medium | high   TYPE: soft | round | dry | hard

BALANCE:
good | fair | unbalanced (excess: alcohol - acid - tannin - sugar)

FLAVOR INTENSITY:
low | moderate | flavorful | powerful

FLAVORS:

FINISH:
short (< 3 sec) | medium (4-5) | long (5-7) | v. long (>8 sec)

CONCLUSION:

STYLE:
traditional | in-between | modern

rating: ☆ ☆ ☆ ☆ ☆

FOOD: **FOOD PAIRING:**

MATCH: perfect | good | neutral | bad

tasting date: location:

tasting partner(s):

wine name:

producer:

region/appellation:

grape varieties:

vintage: alcohol: price:

COLOR DEPTH:
watery | pale | medium | deep | dark

COLOR HUE:
WHITE: greenish | yellow | straw yellow | gold | amber
RED: purplish | ruby | red | garnet | brick | brown
ROSÉ: pink | salmon | orange | copper

CLARITY:
clear | slight haze | cloudy

AROMA INTENSITY:
low | moderate | aromatic | powerful

DEVELOPMENT:
youthful | some age | aged

AROMAS:

DRY/SWEET:
bone dry | dry | off dry | medium sweet | sweet | very sweet

BODY:
very light | light | medium | medium-full | full-bodied | heavy

ACIDITY:
tart | crisp | fresh | smooth | flabby

TANNINS (IF PRESENT):
LEVEL: low | medium | high   TYPE: soft | round | dry | hard

BALANCE:
good | fair | unbalanced (excess: alcohol - acid - tannin - sugar)

FLAVOR INTENSITY:
low | moderate | flavorful | powerful

FLAVORS:

FINISH:
short (< 3 sec) | medium (4-5) | long (5-7) | v. long (>8 sec)

CONCLUSION:

STYLE:
traditional | in-between | modern

rating: ☆ ☆ ☆ ☆ ☆

FOOD: **FOOD PAIRING:**
                MATCH: perfect | good | neutral | bad

tasting date: location:

tasting partner(s):

wine name:

producer:

region/appellation:

grape varieties:

vintage: alcohol: price:

COLOR DEPTH:
watery | pale | medium | deep | dark

COLOR HUE:
WHITE: greenish | yellow | straw yellow | gold | amber
RED: purplish | ruby | red | garnet | brick | brown
ROSÉ: pink | salmon | orange | copper

CLARITY:
clear | slight haze | cloudy

AROMA INTENSITY:
low | moderate | aromatic | powerful

DEVELOPMENT:
youthful | some age | aged

AROMAS:

DRY/SWEET:
bone dry | dry | off dry | medium sweet | sweet | very sweet

BODY:
very light | light | medium | medium-full | full-bodied | heavy

ACIDITY:
tart | crisp | fresh | smooth | flabby

TANNINS (IF PRESENT):
LEVEL: low | medium | high   TYPE: soft | round | dry | hard

BALANCE:
good | fair | unbalanced (excess: alcohol - acid - tannin - sugar)

FLAVOR INTENSITY:
low | moderate | flavorful | powerful

FLAVORS:

FINISH:
short (< 3 sec) | medium (4-5) | long (5-7) | v. long (>8 sec)

CONCLUSION:

STYLE:
traditional | in-between | modern

rating: ☆ ☆ ☆ ☆ ☆

FOOD: ## FOOD PAIRING:
MATCH: perfect | good | neutral | bad

tasting date: location:

tasting partner(s):

wine name:

producer:

region/appellation:

grape varieties:

vintage: alcohol: price:

COLOR DEPTH:
watery | pale | medium | deep | dark

COLOR HUE:
WHITE: greenish | yellow | straw yellow | gold | amber
RED: purplish | ruby | red | garnet | brick | brown
ROSÉ: pink | salmon | orange | copper

CLARITY:
clear | slight haze | cloudy

AROMA INTENSITY:
low | moderate | aromatic | powerful

DEVELOPMENT:
youthful | some age | aged

AROMAS:

DRY/SWEET:
bone dry | dry | off dry | medium sweet | sweet | very sweet

BODY:
very light | light | medium | medium-full | full-bodied | heavy

ACIDITY:
tart | crisp | fresh | smooth | flabby

TANNINS (IF PRESENT):
LEVEL: low | medium | high   TYPE: soft | round | dry | hard

BALANCE:
good | fair | unbalanced (excess: alcohol - acid - tannin - sugar)

FLAVOR INTENSITY:
low | moderate | flavorful | powerful

FLAVORS:

FINISH:
short (< 3 sec) | medium (4-5) | long (5-7) | v. long (>8 sec)

CONCLUSION:

STYLE:
traditional | in-between | modern

rating: ☆ ☆ ☆ ☆ ☆

FOOD: **FOOD PAIRING:**
               MATCH: perfect | good | neutral | bad

tasting date: location:

tasting partner(s):

wine name:

producer:

region/appellation:

grape varieties:

vintage: alcohol: price:

COLOR DEPTH:
watery | pale | medium | deep | dark

COLOR HUE:
WHITE: greenish | yellow | straw yellow | gold | amber
RED: purplish | ruby | red | garnet | brick | brown
ROSÉ: pink | salmon | orange | copper

CLARITY:
clear | slight haze | cloudy

AROMA INTENSITY:
low | moderate | aromatic | powerful

DEVELOPMENT:
youthful | some age | aged

AROMAS:

DRY/SWEET:
bone dry | dry | off dry | medium sweet | sweet | very sweet

BODY:
very light | light | medium | medium-full | full-bodied | heavy

ACIDITY:
tart | crisp | fresh | smooth | flabby

TANNINS (IF PRESENT):
LEVEL: low | medium | high   TYPE: soft | round | dry | hard

BALANCE:
good | fair | unbalanced (excess: alcohol - acid - tannin - sugar)

FLAVOR INTENSITY:
low | moderate | flavorful | powerful

FLAVORS:

FINISH:
short (< 3 sec) | medium (4-5) | long (5-7) | v. long (>8 sec)

CONCLUSION:

STYLE:
traditional | in-between | modern

rating: ☆ ☆ ☆ ☆ ☆

FOOD: ## FOOD PAIRING:
                   MATCH: perfect | good | neutral | bad

tasting date: location:

tasting partner(s):

wine name:

producer:

region/appellation:

grape varieties:

vintage: alcohol: price:

COLOR DEPTH:
watery | pale | medium | deep | dark

COLOR HUE:
WHITE: greenish | yellow | straw yellow | gold | amber
RED: purplish | ruby | red | garnet | brick | brown
ROSÉ: pink | salmon | orange | copper

CLARITY:
clear | slight haze | cloudy

AROMA INTENSITY:
low | moderate | aromatic | powerful

DEVELOPMENT:
youthful | some age | aged

AROMAS:

DRY/SWEET:
bone dry | dry | off dry | medium sweet | sweet | very sweet

BODY:
very light | light | medium | medium-full | full-bodied | heavy

ACIDITY:
tart | crisp | fresh | smooth | flabby

TANNINS (IF PRESENT):
LEVEL: low | medium | high   TYPE: soft | round | dry | hard

BALANCE:
good | fair | unbalanced (excess: alcohol - acid - tannin - sugar)

FLAVOR INTENSITY:
low | moderate | flavorful | powerful

FLAVORS:

FINISH:
short (< 3 sec) | medium (4-5) | long (5-7) | v. long (>8 sec)

CONCLUSION:

STYLE:
traditional | in-between | modern

rating: ☆ ☆ ☆ ☆ ☆

FOOD: **FOOD PAIRING:**

MATCH: perfect | good | neutral | bad

tasting date: location:

tasting partner(s):

wine name:

producer:

region/appellation:

grape varieties:

vintage: alcohol: price:

COLOR DEPTH:
watery | pale | medium | deep | dark

COLOR HUE:
WHITE: greenish | yellow | straw yellow | gold | amber
RED: purplish | ruby | red | garnet | brick | brown
ROSÉ: pink | salmon | orange | copper

CLARITY:
clear | slight haze | cloudy

AROMA INTENSITY:
low | moderate | aromatic | powerful

DEVELOPMENT:
youthful | some age | aged

AROMAS:

DRY/SWEET:
bone dry | dry | off dry | medium sweet | sweet | very sweet

BODY:
very light | light | medium | medium-full | full-bodied | heavy

ACIDITY:
tart | crisp | fresh | smooth | flabby

TANNINS (IF PRESENT):
LEVEL: low | medium | high   TYPE: soft | round | dry | hard

BALANCE:
good | fair | unbalanced (excess: alcohol - acid - tannin - sugar)

FLAVOR INTENSITY:
low | moderate | flavorful | powerful

FLAVORS:

FINISH:
short (< 3 sec) | medium (4-5) | long (5-7) | v. long (>8 sec)

CONCLUSION:

STYLE:
traditional | in-between | modern

rating: ☆ ☆ ☆ ☆ ☆

FOOD: **FOOD PAIRING:**
MATCH: perfect | good | neutral | bad

tasting date: location:

tasting partner(s):

wine name:

producer:

region/appellation:

grape varieties:

vintage: alcohol: price:

COLOR DEPTH:
watery | pale | medium | deep | dark

COLOR HUE:
WHITE: greenish | yellow | straw yellow | gold | amber
RED: purplish | ruby | red | garnet | brick | brown
ROSÉ: pink | salmon | orange | copper

CLARITY:
clear | slight haze | cloudy

AROMA INTENSITY:
low | moderate | aromatic | powerful

DEVELOPMENT:
youthful | some age | aged

AROMAS:

DRY/SWEET:
bone dry | dry | off dry | medium sweet | sweet | very sweet

BODY:
very light | light | medium | medium-full | full-bodied | heavy

ACIDITY:
tart | crisp | fresh | smooth | flabby

TANNINS (IF PRESENT):
LEVEL: low | medium | high   TYPE: soft | round | dry | hard

BALANCE:
good | fair | unbalanced (excess: alcohol - acid - tannin - sugar)

FLAVOR INTENSITY:
low | moderate | flavorful | powerful

FLAVORS:

FINISH:
short (< 3 sec) | medium (4-5) | long (5-7) | v. long (>8 sec)

CONCLUSION:

STYLE:
traditional | in-between | modern

rating: ☆ ☆ ☆ ☆ ☆

FOOD: **FOOD PAIRING:**

MATCH: perfect | good | neutral | bad

tasting date: location:

tasting partner(s):

wine name:

producer:

region/appellation:

grape varieties:

vintage: alcohol: price:

COLOR DEPTH:
watery | pale | medium | deep | dark

COLOR HUE:
WHITE: greenish | yellow | straw yellow | gold | amber
RED: purplish | ruby | red | garnet | brick | brown
ROSÉ: pink | salmon | orange | copper

CLARITY:
clear | slight haze | cloudy

AROMA INTENSITY:
low | moderate | aromatic | powerful

DEVELOPMENT:
youthful | some age | aged

AROMAS:

DRY/SWEET:
bone dry | dry | off dry | medium sweet | sweet | very sweet

BODY:
very light | light | medium | medium-full | full-bodied | heavy

ACIDITY:
tart | crisp | fresh | smooth | flabby

TANNINS (IF PRESENT):
LEVEL: low | medium | high   TYPE: soft | round | dry | hard

BALANCE:
good | fair | unbalanced (excess: alcohol - acid - tannin - sugar)

FLAVOR INTENSITY:
low | moderate | flavorful | powerful

FLAVORS:

FINISH:
short (< 3 sec) | medium (4-5) | long (5-7) | v. long (>8 sec)

CONCLUSION:

STYLE:
traditional | in-between | modern

rating: ☆☆☆☆☆

FOOD: **FOOD PAIRING:**

                  MATCH: perfect | good | neutral | bad

tasting date: location:

tasting partner(s):

wine name:

producer:

region/appellation:

grape varieties:

vintage: alcohol: price:

COLOR DEPTH:
watery | pale | medium | deep | dark

COLOR HUE:
WHITE: greenish | yellow | straw yellow | gold | amber
RED: purplish | ruby | red | garnet | brick | brown
ROSÉ: pink | salmon | orange | copper

CLARITY:
clear | slight haze | cloudy

AROMA INTENSITY:
low | moderate | aromatic | powerful

DEVELOPMENT:
youthful | some age | aged

AROMAS:

DRY/SWEET:
bone dry | dry | off dry | medium sweet | sweet | very sweet

BODY:
very light | light | medium | medium-full | full-bodied | heavy

ACIDITY:
tart | crisp | fresh | smooth | flabby

TANNINS (IF PRESENT):
LEVEL: low | medium | high   TYPE: soft | round | dry | hard

BALANCE:
good | fair | unbalanced (excess: alcohol - acid - tannin - sugar)

FLAVOR INTENSITY:
low | moderate | flavorful | powerful

FLAVORS:

FINISH:
short (< 3 sec) | medium (4-5) | long (5-7) | v. long (>8 sec)

CONCLUSION:

STYLE:
traditional | in-between | modern

rating: ☆ ☆ ☆ ☆ ☆

FOOD: ### FOOD PAIRING:
MATCH: perfect | good | neutral | bad

tasting date: location:

tasting partner(s):

wine name:

producer:

region/appellation:

grape varieties:

vintage: alcohol: price:

COLOR DEPTH:
watery | pale | medium | deep | dark

COLOR HUE:
WHITE: greenish | yellow | straw yellow | gold | amber
RED: purplish | ruby | red | garnet | brick | brown
ROSÉ: pink | salmon | orange | copper

CLARITY:
clear | slight haze | cloudy

AROMA INTENSITY:
low | moderate | aromatic | powerful

DEVELOPMENT:
youthful | some age | aged

AROMAS:

DRY/SWEET:
bone dry | dry | off dry | medium sweet | sweet | very sweet

BODY:
very light | light | medium | medium-full | full-bodied | heavy

ACIDITY:
tart | crisp | fresh | smooth | flabby

TANNINS (IF PRESENT):
LEVEL: low | medium | high   TYPE: soft | round | dry | hard

BALANCE:
good | fair | unbalanced (excess: alcohol - acid - tannin - sugar)

FLAVOR INTENSITY:
low | moderate | flavorful | powerful

FLAVORS:

FINISH:
short (< 3 sec) | medium (4-5) | long (5-7) | v. long (>8 sec)

CONCLUSION:

STYLE:
traditional | in-between | modern

rating: ☆ ☆ ☆ ☆ ☆

FOOD: **FOOD PAIRING:**

MATCH: perfect | good | neutral | bad

tasting date: location:

tasting partner(s):

wine name:

producer:

region/appellation:

grape varieties:

vintage: alcohol: price:

COLOR DEPTH:
watery | pale | medium | deep | dark
COLOR HUE:
WHITE: greenish | yellow | straw yellow | gold | amber
RED: purplish | ruby | red | garnet | brick | brown
ROSÉ: pink | salmon | orange | copper
CLARITY:
clear | slight haze | cloudy

AROMA INTENSITY:
low | moderate | aromatic | powerful
DEVELOPMENT:
youthful | some age | aged
AROMAS:

DRY/SWEET:
bone dry | dry | off dry | medium sweet | sweet | very sweet
BODY:
very light | light | medium | medium-full | full-bodied | heavy
ACIDITY:
tart | crisp | fresh | smooth | flabby
TANNINS (IF PRESENT):
LEVEL: low | medium | high   TYPE: soft | round | dry | hard
BALANCE:
good | fair | unbalanced (excess: alcohol - acid - tannin - sugar)
FLAVOR INTENSITY:
low | moderate | flavorful | powerful
FLAVORS:

FINISH:
short (< 3 sec) | medium (4-5) | long (5-7) | v. long (>8 sec)
CONCLUSION:

STYLE:
traditional | in-between | modern
rating: ☆ ☆ ☆ ☆ ☆

FOOD: **FOOD PAIRING:**
                    MATCH: perfect | good | neutral | bad

tasting date: location:

tasting partner(s):

wine name:

producer:

region/appellation:

grape varieties:

vintage: alcohol: price:

COLOR DEPTH:
watery | pale | medium | deep | dark

COLOR HUE:
WHITE: greenish | yellow | straw yellow | gold | amber
RED: purplish | ruby | red | garnet | brick | brown
ROSÉ: pink | salmon | orange | copper

CLARITY:
clear | slight haze | cloudy

AROMA INTENSITY:
low | moderate | aromatic | powerful

DEVELOPMENT:
youthful | some age | aged

AROMAS:

DRY/SWEET:
bone dry | dry | off dry | medium sweet | sweet | very sweet

BODY:
very light | light | medium | medium-full | full-bodied | heavy

ACIDITY:
tart | crisp | fresh | smooth | flabby

TANNINS (IF PRESENT):
LEVEL: low | medium | high   TYPE: soft | round | dry | hard

BALANCE:
good | fair | unbalanced (excess: alcohol - acid - tannin - sugar)

FLAVOR INTENSITY:
low | moderate | flavorful | powerful

FLAVORS:

FINISH:
short (< 3 sec) | medium (4-5) | long (5-7) | v. long (>8 sec)

CONCLUSION:

STYLE:
traditional | in-between | modern

rating: ☆☆☆☆☆

FOOD: **FOOD PAIRING:**

MATCH: perfect | good | neutral | bad

tasting date: location:

tasting partner(s):

wine name:

producer:

region/appellation:

grape varieties:

vintage: alcohol: price:

COLOR DEPTH:
watery | pale | medium | deep | dark

COLOR HUE:
WHITE: greenish | yellow | straw yellow | gold | amber
RED: purplish | ruby | red | garnet | brick | brown
ROSÉ: pink | salmon | orange | copper

CLARITY:
clear | slight haze | cloudy

AROMA INTENSITY:
low | moderate | aromatic | powerful

DEVELOPMENT:
youthful | some age | aged

AROMAS:

DRY/SWEET:
bone dry | dry | off dry | medium sweet | sweet | very sweet

BODY:
very light | light | medium | medium-full | full-bodied | heavy

ACIDITY:
tart | crisp | fresh | smooth | flabby

TANNINS (IF PRESENT):
LEVEL: low | medium | high   TYPE: soft | round | dry | hard

BALANCE:
good | fair | unbalanced (excess: alcohol - acid - tannin - sugar)

FLAVOR INTENSITY:
low | moderate | flavorful | powerful

FLAVORS:

FINISH:
short (< 3 sec) | medium (4-5) | long (5-7) | v. long (>8 sec)

CONCLUSION:

STYLE:
traditional | in-between | modern

rating: ☆ ☆ ☆ ☆ ☆

FOOD: **FOOD PAIRING:**
MATCH: perfect | good | neutral | bad

tasting date: location:

tasting partner(s):

wine name:

producer:

region/appellation:

grape varieties:

vintage: alcohol: price:

COLOR DEPTH:
watery | pale | medium | deep | dark

COLOR HUE:
WHITE: greenish | yellow | straw yellow | gold | amber
RED: purplish | ruby | red | garnet | brick | brown
ROSÉ: pink | salmon | orange | copper

CLARITY:
clear | slight haze | cloudy

AROMA INTENSITY:
low | moderate | aromatic | powerful

DEVELOPMENT:
youthful | some age | aged

AROMAS:

DRY/SWEET:
bone dry | dry | off dry | medium sweet | sweet | very sweet

BODY:
very light | light | medium | medium-full | full-bodied | heavy

ACIDITY:
tart | crisp | fresh | smooth | flabby

TANNINS (IF PRESENT):
LEVEL: low | medium | high   TYPE: soft | round | dry | hard

BALANCE:
good | fair | unbalanced (excess: alcohol - acid - tannin - sugar)

FLAVOR INTENSITY:
low | moderate | flavorful | powerful

FLAVORS:

FINISH:
short (< 3 sec) | medium (4-5) | long (5-7) | v. long (>8 sec)

CONCLUSION:

STYLE:
traditional | in-between | modern

rating: ☆ ☆ ☆ ☆ ☆

FOOD:

FOOD PAIRING:
MATCH: perfect | good | neutral | bad

tasting date: location:

tasting partner(s):

wine name:

producer:

region/appellation:

grape varieties:

vintage: alcohol: price:

 COLOR DEPTH:
watery | pale | medium | deep | dark

COLOR HUE:
WHITE: greenish | yellow | straw yellow | gold | amber
RED: purplish | ruby | red | garnet | brick | brown
ROSÉ: pink | salmon | orange | copper

CLARITY:
clear | slight haze | cloudy

 AROMA INTENSITY:
low | moderate | aromatic | powerful

DEVELOPMENT:
youthful | some age | aged

AROMAS:

 DRY/SWEET:
bone dry | dry | off dry | medium sweet | sweet | very sweet

BODY:
very light | light | medium | medium-full | full-bodied | heavy

ACIDITY:
tart | crisp | fresh | smooth | flabby

TANNINS (IF PRESENT):
LEVEL: low | medium | high   TYPE: soft | round | dry | hard

BALANCE:
good | fair | unbalanced (excess: alcohol - acid - tannin - sugar)

FLAVOR INTENSITY:
low | moderate | flavorful | powerful

FLAVORS:

FINISH:
short (< 3 sec) | medium (4-5) | long (5-7) | v. long (>8 sec)

CONCLUSION:

STYLE:
traditional | in-between | modern

rating: ☆ ☆ ☆ ☆ ☆

FOOD: **FOOD PAIRING:**
MATCH: perfect | good | neutral | bad

tasting date: location:

tasting partner(s):

wine name:

producer:

region/appellation:

grape varieties:

vintage: alcohol: price:

COLOR DEPTH:
watery | pale | medium | deep | dark

COLOR HUE:
WHITE: greenish | yellow | straw yellow | gold | amber
RED: purplish | ruby | red | garnet | brick | brown
ROSÉ: pink | salmon | orange | copper

CLARITY:
clear | slight haze | cloudy

AROMA INTENSITY:
low | moderate | aromatic | powerful

DEVELOPMENT:
youthful | some age | aged

AROMAS:

DRY/SWEET:
bone dry | dry | off dry | medium sweet | sweet | very sweet

BODY:
very light | light | medium | medium-full | full-bodied | heavy

ACIDITY:
tart | crisp | fresh | smooth | flabby

TANNINS (IF PRESENT):
LEVEL: low | medium | high   TYPE: soft | round | dry | hard

BALANCE:
good | fair | unbalanced (excess: alcohol - acid - tannin - sugar)

FLAVOR INTENSITY:
low | moderate | flavorful | powerful

FLAVORS:

FINISH:
short (< 3 sec) | medium (4-5) | long (5-7) | v. long (>8 sec)

CONCLUSION:

STYLE:
traditional | in-between | modern

rating: ☆ ☆ ☆ ☆ ☆

FOOD: **FOOD PAIRING:**

MATCH: perfect | good | neutral | bad

tasting date: location:

tasting partner(s):

wine name:

producer:

region/appellation:

grape varieties:

vintage: alcohol: price:

COLOR DEPTH:
watery | pale | medium | deep | dark

COLOR HUE:
WHITE: greenish | yellow | straw yellow | gold | amber
RED: purplish | ruby | red | garnet | brick | brown
ROSÉ: pink | salmon | orange | copper

CLARITY:
clear | slight haze | cloudy

AROMA INTENSITY:
low | moderate | aromatic | powerful

DEVELOPMENT:
youthful | some age | aged

AROMAS:

DRY/SWEET:
bone dry | dry | off dry | medium sweet | sweet | very sweet

BODY:
very light | light | medium | medium-full | full-bodied | heavy

ACIDITY:
tart | crisp | fresh | smooth | flabby

TANNINS (IF PRESENT):
LEVEL: low | medium | high   TYPE: soft | round | dry | hard

BALANCE:
good | fair | unbalanced (excess: alcohol - acid - tannin - sugar)

FLAVOR INTENSITY:
low | moderate | flavorful | powerful

FLAVORS:

FINISH:
short (< 3 sec) | medium (4-5) | long (5-7) | v. long (>8 sec)

CONCLUSION:

STYLE:
traditional | in-between | modern

rating: ☆ ☆ ☆ ☆ ☆

FOOD: **FOOD PAIRING:**
MATCH: perfect | good | neutral | bad

tasting date: location:

tasting partner(s):

wine name:

producer:

region/appellation:

grape varieties:

vintage: alcohol: price:

COLOR DEPTH:
watery | pale | medium | deep | dark

COLOR HUE:
WHITE: greenish | yellow | straw yellow | gold | amber
RED: purplish | ruby | red | garnet | brick | brown
ROSÉ: pink | salmon | orange | copper

CLARITY:
clear | slight haze | cloudy

AROMA INTENSITY:
low | moderate | aromatic | powerful

DEVELOPMENT:
youthful | some age | aged

AROMAS:

DRY/SWEET:
bone dry | dry | off dry | medium sweet | sweet | very sweet

BODY:
very light | light | medium | medium-full | full-bodied | heavy

ACIDITY:
tart | crisp | fresh | smooth | flabby

TANNINS (IF PRESENT):
LEVEL: low | medium | high   TYPE: soft | round | dry | hard

BALANCE:
good | fair | unbalanced (excess: alcohol - acid - tannin - sugar)

FLAVOR INTENSITY:
low | moderate | flavorful | powerful

FLAVORS:

FINISH:
short (< 3 sec) | medium (4-5) | long (5-7) | v. long (>8 sec)

CONCLUSION:

STYLE:
traditional | in-between | modern

rating: ☆ ☆ ☆ ☆ ☆

FOOD: **FOOD PAIRING:**

MATCH: perfect | good | neutral | bad

tasting date: location:

tasting partner(s):

wine name:

producer:

region/appellation:

grape varieties:

vintage: alcohol: price:

COLOR DEPTH:
watery | pale | medium | deep | dark

COLOR HUE:
WHITE: greenish | yellow | straw yellow | gold | amber
RED: purplish | ruby | red | garnet | brick | brown
ROSÉ: pink | salmon | orange | copper

CLARITY:
clear | slight haze | cloudy

AROMA INTENSITY:
low | moderate | aromatic | powerful

DEVELOPMENT:
youthful | some age | aged

AROMAS:

DRY/SWEET:
bone dry | dry | off dry | medium sweet | sweet | very sweet

BODY:
very light | light | medium | medium-full | full-bodied | heavy

ACIDITY:
tart | crisp | fresh | smooth | flabby

TANNINS (IF PRESENT):
LEVEL: low | medium | high   TYPE: soft | round | dry | hard

BALANCE:
good | fair | unbalanced (excess: alcohol - acid - tannin - sugar)

FLAVOR INTENSITY:
low | moderate | flavorful | powerful

FLAVORS:

FINISH:
short (< 3 sec) | medium (4-5) | long (5-7) | v. long (>8 sec)

CONCLUSION:

STYLE:
traditional | in-between | modern

rating: ☆ ☆ ☆ ☆ ☆

FOOD: **FOOD PAIRING:**

MATCH: perfect | good | neutral | bad

tasting date: location:

tasting partner(s):

wine name:

producer:

region/appellation:

grape varieties:

vintage: alcohol: price:

COLOR DEPTH:
watery | pale | medium | deep | dark

COLOR HUE:
WHITE: greenish | yellow | straw yellow | gold | amber
RED: purplish | ruby | red | garnet | brick | brown
ROSÉ: pink | salmon | orange | copper

CLARITY:
clear | slight haze | cloudy

AROMA INTENSITY:
low | moderate | aromatic | powerful

DEVELOPMENT:
youthful | some age | aged

AROMAS:

DRY/SWEET:
bone dry | dry | off dry | medium sweet | sweet | very sweet

BODY:
very light | light | medium | medium-full | full-bodied | heavy

ACIDITY:
tart | crisp | fresh | smooth | flabby

TANNINS (IF PRESENT):
LEVEL: low | medium | high   TYPE: soft | round | dry | hard

BALANCE:
good | fair | unbalanced (excess: alcohol - acid - tannin - sugar)

FLAVOR INTENSITY:
low | moderate | flavorful | powerful

FLAVORS:

FINISH:
short (< 3 sec) | medium (4-5) | long (5-7) | v. long (>8 sec)

CONCLUSION:

STYLE:
traditional | in-between | modern

rating: ☆ ☆ ☆ ☆ ☆

FOOD: **FOOD PAIRING:**

MATCH: perfect | good | neutral | bad

tasting date: location:

tasting partner(s):

wine name:

producer:

region/appellation:

grape varieties:

vintage: alcohol: price:

COLOR DEPTH:
watery | pale | medium | deep | dark

COLOR HUE:
WHITE: greenish | yellow | straw yellow | gold | amber
RED: purplish | ruby | red | garnet | brick | brown
ROSÉ: pink | salmon | orange | copper

CLARITY:
clear | slight haze | cloudy

AROMA INTENSITY:
low | moderate | aromatic | powerful

DEVELOPMENT:
youthful | some age | aged

AROMAS:

DRY/SWEET:
bone dry | dry | off dry | medium sweet | sweet | very sweet

BODY:
very light | light | medium | medium-full | full-bodied | heavy

ACIDITY:
tart | crisp | fresh | smooth | flabby

TANNINS (IF PRESENT):
LEVEL: low | medium | high   TYPE: soft | round | dry | hard

BALANCE:
good | fair | unbalanced (excess: alcohol - acid - tannin - sugar)

FLAVOR INTENSITY:
low | moderate | flavorful | powerful

FLAVORS:

FINISH:
short (< 3 sec) | medium (4-5) | long (5-7) | v. long (>8 sec)

CONCLUSION:

STYLE:
traditional | in-between | modern

rating: ☆ ☆ ☆ ☆ ☆

FOOD: ## FOOD PAIRING:
MATCH: perfect | good | neutral | bad

tasting date: location:

tasting partner(s):

wine name:

producer:

region/appellation:

grape varieties:

vintage: alcohol: price:

COLOR DEPTH:
watery | pale | medium | deep | dark

COLOR HUE:
WHITE: greenish | yellow | straw yellow | gold | amber
RED: purplish | ruby | red | garnet | brick | brown
ROSÉ: pink | salmon | orange | copper

CLARITY:
clear | slight haze | cloudy

AROMA INTENSITY:
low | moderate | aromatic | powerful

DEVELOPMENT:
youthful | some age | aged

AROMAS:

DRY/SWEET:
bone dry | dry | off dry | medium sweet | sweet | very sweet

BODY:
very light | light | medium | medium-full | full-bodied | heavy

ACIDITY:
tart | crisp | fresh | smooth | flabby

TANNINS (IF PRESENT):
LEVEL: low | medium | high   TYPE: soft | round | dry | hard

BALANCE:
good | fair | unbalanced (excess: alcohol - acid - tannin - sugar)

FLAVOR INTENSITY:
low | moderate | flavorful | powerful

FLAVORS:

FINISH:
short (< 3 sec) | medium (4-5) | long (5-7) | v. long (>8 sec)

CONCLUSION:

STYLE:
traditional | in-between | modern

rating: ☆ ☆ ☆ ☆ ☆

FOOD: **FOOD PAIRING:**

MATCH: perfect | good | neutral | bad

tasting date: location:

tasting partner(s):

wine name:

producer:

region/appellation:

grape varieties:

vintage: alcohol: price:

COLOR DEPTH:
watery | pale | medium | deep | dark

COLOR HUE:
WHITE: greenish | yellow | straw yellow | gold | amber
RED: purplish | ruby | red | garnet | brick | brown
ROSÉ: pink | salmon | orange | copper

CLARITY:
clear | slight haze | cloudy

AROMA INTENSITY:
low | moderate | aromatic | powerful

DEVELOPMENT:
youthful | some age | aged

AROMAS:

DRY/SWEET:
bone dry | dry | off dry | medium sweet | sweet | very sweet

BODY:
very light | light | medium | medium-full | full-bodied | heavy

ACIDITY:
tart | crisp | fresh | smooth | flabby

TANNINS (IF PRESENT):
LEVEL: low | medium | high   TYPE: soft | round | dry | hard

BALANCE:
good | fair | unbalanced (excess: alcohol - acid - tannin - sugar)

FLAVOR INTENSITY:
low | moderate | flavorful | powerful

FLAVORS:

FINISH:
short (< 3 sec) | medium (4-5) | long (5-7) | v. long (>8 sec)

CONCLUSION:

STYLE:
traditional | in-between | modern

rating: ☆ ☆ ☆ ☆ ☆

FOOD: ## FOOD PAIRING:
MATCH: perfect | good | neutral | bad

tasting date: location:

tasting partner(s):

wine name:

producer:

region/appellation:

grape varieties:

vintage: alcohol: price:

COLOR DEPTH:
watery | pale | medium | deep | dark
COLOR HUE:
WHITE: greenish | yellow | straw yellow | gold | amber
RED: purplish | ruby | red | garnet | brick | brown
ROSÉ: pink | salmon | orange | copper
CLARITY:
clear | slight haze | cloudy

AROMA INTENSITY:
low | moderate | aromatic | powerful
DEVELOPMENT:
youthful | some age | aged
AROMAS:

DRY/SWEET:
bone dry | dry | off dry | medium sweet | sweet | very sweet
BODY:
very light | light | medium | medium-full | full-bodied | heavy
ACIDITY:
tart | crisp | fresh | smooth | flabby
TANNINS (IF PRESENT):
LEVEL: low | medium | high   TYPE: soft | round | dry | hard
BALANCE:
good | fair | unbalanced (excess: alcohol - acid - tannin - sugar)
FLAVOR INTENSITY:
low | moderate | flavorful | powerful
FLAVORS:

FINISH:
short (< 3 sec) | medium (4-5) | long (5-7) | v. long (>8 sec)
CONCLUSION:

STYLE:
traditional | in-between | modern
rating: ☆ ☆ ☆ ☆ ☆

FOOD: **FOOD PAIRING:**
MATCH: perfect | good | neutral | bad

tasting date: location:

tasting partner(s):

wine name:

producer:

region/appellation:

grape varieties:

vintage: alcohol: price:

COLOR DEPTH:
watery | pale | medium | deep | dark

COLOR HUE:
WHITE: greenish | yellow | straw yellow | gold | amber
RED: purplish | ruby | red | garnet | brick | brown
ROSÉ: pink | salmon | orange | copper

CLARITY:
clear | slight haze | cloudy

AROMA INTENSITY:
low | moderate | aromatic | powerful

DEVELOPMENT:
youthful | some age | aged

AROMAS:

DRY/SWEET:
bone dry | dry | off dry | medium sweet | sweet | very sweet

BODY:
very light | light | medium | medium-full | full-bodied | heavy

ACIDITY:
tart | crisp | fresh | smooth | flabby

TANNINS (IF PRESENT):
LEVEL: low | medium | high   TYPE: soft | round | dry | hard

BALANCE:
good | fair | unbalanced (excess: alcohol - acid - tannin - sugar)

FLAVOR INTENSITY:
low | moderate | flavorful | powerful

FLAVORS:

FINISH:
short (< 3 sec) | medium (4-5) | long (5-7) | v. long (>8 sec)

CONCLUSION:

STYLE:
traditional | in-between | modern

rating: ☆ ☆ ☆ ☆ ☆

FOOD: **FOOD PAIRING:**

MATCH: perfect | good | neutral | bad

tasting date: location:

tasting partner(s):

wine name:

producer:

region/appellation:

grape varieties:

vintage: alcohol: price:

COLOR DEPTH:
watery | pale | medium | deep | dark
COLOR HUE:
WHITE: greenish | yellow | straw yellow | gold | amber
RED: purplish | ruby | red | garnet | brick | brown
ROSÉ: pink | salmon | orange | copper

CLARITY:
clear | slight haze | cloudy

AROMA INTENSITY:
low | moderate | aromatic | powerful
DEVELOPMENT:
youthful | some age | aged
AROMAS:

DRY/SWEET:
bone dry | dry | off dry | medium sweet | sweet | very sweet
BODY:
very light | light | medium | medium-full | full-bodied | heavy
ACIDITY:
tart | crisp | fresh | smooth | flabby
TANNINS (IF PRESENT):
LEVEL: low | medium | high   TYPE: soft | round | dry | hard
BALANCE:
good | fair | unbalanced (excess: alcohol - acid - tannin - sugar)
FLAVOR INTENSITY:
low | moderate | flavorful | powerful
FLAVORS:

FINISH:
short (< 3 sec) | medium (4-5) | long (5-7) | v. long (>8 sec)
CONCLUSION:

STYLE:
traditional | in-between | modern

rating: ☆ ☆ ☆ ☆ ☆

FOOD: **FOOD PAIRING:**

MATCH: perfect | good | neutral | bad

tasting date: location:

tasting partner(s):

wine name:

producer:

region/appellation:

grape varieties:

vintage: alcohol: price:

COLOR DEPTH:
watery | pale | medium | deep | dark

COLOR HUE:
WHITE: greenish | yellow | straw yellow | gold | amber
RED: purplish | ruby | red | garnet | brick | brown
ROSÉ: pink | salmon | orange | copper

CLARITY:
clear | slight haze | cloudy

AROMA INTENSITY:
low | moderate | aromatic | powerful

DEVELOPMENT:
youthful | some age | aged

AROMAS:

DRY/SWEET:
bone dry | dry | off dry | medium sweet | sweet | very sweet

BODY:
very light | light | medium | medium-full | full-bodied | heavy

ACIDITY:
tart | crisp | fresh | smooth | flabby

TANNINS (IF PRESENT):
LEVEL: low | medium | high   TYPE: soft | round | dry | hard

BALANCE:
good | fair | unbalanced (excess: alcohol - acid - tannin - sugar)

FLAVOR INTENSITY:
low | moderate | flavorful | powerful

FLAVORS:

FINISH:
short (< 3 sec) | medium (4-5) | long (5-7) | v. long (>8 sec)

CONCLUSION:

STYLE:
traditional | in-between | modern

rating: ☆ ☆ ☆ ☆ ☆

FOOD: **FOOD PAIRING:**

                MATCH: perfect | good | neutral | bad

tasting date: location:

tasting partner(s):

wine name:

producer:

region/appellation:

grape varieties:

vintage: alcohol: price:

COLOR DEPTH:
watery | pale | medium | deep | dark

COLOR HUE:
WHITE: greenish | yellow | straw yellow | gold | amber
RED: purplish | ruby | red | garnet | brick | brown
ROSÉ: pink | salmon | orange | copper

CLARITY:
clear | slight haze | cloudy

AROMA INTENSITY:
low | moderate | aromatic | powerful

DEVELOPMENT:
youthful | some age | aged

AROMAS:

DRY/SWEET:
bone dry | dry | off dry | medium sweet | sweet | very sweet

BODY:
very light | light | medium | medium-full | full-bodied | heavy

ACIDITY:
tart | crisp | fresh | smooth | flabby

TANNINS (IF PRESENT):
LEVEL: low | medium | high   TYPE: soft | round | dry | hard

BALANCE:
good | fair | unbalanced (excess: alcohol - acid - tannin - sugar)

FLAVOR INTENSITY:
low | moderate | flavorful | powerful

FLAVORS:

FINISH:
short (< 3 sec) | medium (4-5) | long (5-7) | v. long (>8 sec)

CONCLUSION:

STYLE:
traditional | in-between | modern

rating: ☆ ☆ ☆ ☆ ☆

FOOD: ## FOOD PAIRING:
MATCH: perfect | good | neutral | bad

tasting date: location:

tasting partner(s):

wine name:

producer:

region/appellation:

grape varieties:

vintage: alcohol: price:

COLOR DEPTH:
watery | pale | medium | deep | dark

COLOR HUE:
WHITE: greenish | yellow | straw yellow | gold | amber
RED: purplish | ruby | red | garnet | brick | brown
ROSÉ: pink | salmon | orange | copper

CLARITY:
clear | slight haze | cloudy

AROMA INTENSITY:
low | moderate | aromatic | powerful

DEVELOPMENT:
youthful | some age | aged

AROMAS:

DRY/SWEET:
bone dry | dry | off dry | medium sweet | sweet | very sweet

BODY:
very light | light | medium | medium-full | full-bodied | heavy

ACIDITY:
tart | crisp | fresh | smooth | flabby

TANNINS (IF PRESENT):
LEVEL: low | medium | high   TYPE: soft | round | dry | hard

BALANCE:
good | fair | unbalanced (excess: alcohol - acid - tannin - sugar)

FLAVOR INTENSITY:
low | moderate | flavorful | powerful

FLAVORS:

FINISH:
short (< 3 sec) | medium (4-5) | long (5-7) | v. long (>8 sec)

CONCLUSION:

STYLE:
traditional | in-between | modern

rating: ☆ ☆ ☆ ☆ ☆

FOOD: **FOOD PAIRING:**

MATCH: perfect | good | neutral | bad

tasting date: location:

tasting partner(s):

wine name:

producer:

region/appellation:

grape varieties:

vintage: alcohol: price:

COLOR DEPTH:
watery | pale | medium | deep | dark

COLOR HUE:
WHITE: greenish | yellow | straw yellow | gold | amber
RED: purplish | ruby | red | garnet | brick | brown
ROSÉ: pink | salmon | orange | copper

CLARITY:
clear | slight haze | cloudy

AROMA INTENSITY:
low | moderate | aromatic | powerful

DEVELOPMENT:
youthful | some age | aged

AROMAS:

DRY/SWEET:
bone dry | dry | off dry | medium sweet | sweet | very sweet

BODY:
very light | light | medium | medium-full | full-bodied | heavy

ACIDITY:
tart | crisp | fresh | smooth | flabby

TANNINS (IF PRESENT):
LEVEL: low | medium | high   TYPE: soft | round | dry | hard

BALANCE:
good | fair | unbalanced (excess: alcohol - acid - tannin - sugar)

FLAVOR INTENSITY:
low | moderate | flavorful | powerful

FLAVORS:

FINISH:
short (< 3 sec) | medium (4-5) | long (5-7) | v. long (>8 sec)

CONCLUSION:

STYLE:
traditional | in-between | modern

rating: ☆ ☆ ☆ ☆ ☆

FOOD: **FOOD PAIRING:**

MATCH: perfect | good | neutral | bad

tasting date: location:

tasting partner(s):

wine name:

producer:

region/appellation:

grape varieties:

vintage: alcohol: price:

COLOR DEPTH:
watery | pale | medium | deep | dark

COLOR HUE:
WHITE: greenish | yellow | straw yellow | gold | amber
RED: purplish | ruby | red | garnet | brick | brown
ROSÉ: pink | salmon | orange | copper

CLARITY:
clear | slight haze | cloudy

AROMA INTENSITY:
low | moderate | aromatic | powerful

DEVELOPMENT:
youthful | some age | aged

AROMAS:

DRY/SWEET:
bone dry | dry | off dry | medium sweet | sweet | very sweet

BODY:
very light | light | medium | medium-full | full-bodied | heavy

ACIDITY:
tart | crisp | fresh | smooth | flabby

TANNINS (IF PRESENT):
LEVEL: low | medium | high   TYPE: soft | round | dry | hard

BALANCE:
good | fair | unbalanced (excess: alcohol - acid - tannin - sugar)

FLAVOR INTENSITY:
low | moderate | flavorful | powerful

FLAVORS:

FINISH:
short (< 3 sec) | medium (4-5) | long (5-7) | v. long (>8 sec)

CONCLUSION:

STYLE:
traditional | in-between | modern

rating: ☆ ☆ ☆ ☆ ☆

FOOD: **FOOD PAIRING:**
                  MATCH: perfect | good | neutral | bad

tasting date: location:

tasting partner(s):

wine name:

producer:

region/appellation:

grape varieties:

vintage: alcohol: price:

COLOR DEPTH:
watery | pale | medium | deep | dark

COLOR HUE:
WHITE: greenish | yellow | straw yellow | gold | amber
RED: purplish | ruby | red | garnet | brick | brown
ROSÉ: pink | salmon | orange | copper

CLARITY:
clear | slight haze | cloudy

AROMA INTENSITY:
low | moderate | aromatic | powerful

DEVELOPMENT:
youthful | some age | aged

AROMAS:

DRY/SWEET:
bone dry | dry | off dry | medium sweet | sweet | very sweet

BODY:
very light | light | medium | medium-full | full-bodied | heavy

ACIDITY:
tart | crisp | fresh | smooth | flabby

TANNINS (IF PRESENT):
LEVEL: low | medium | high   TYPE: soft | round | dry | hard

BALANCE:
good | fair | unbalanced (excess: alcohol - acid - tannin - sugar)

FLAVOR INTENSITY:
low | moderate | flavorful | powerful

FLAVORS:

FINISH:
short (< 3 sec) | medium (4-5) | long (5-7) | v. long (>8 sec)

CONCLUSION:

STYLE:
traditional | in-between | modern

rating: ☆ ☆ ☆ ☆ ☆

FOOD: **FOOD PAIRING:**

MATCH: perfect | good | neutral | bad

tasting date: location:

tasting partner(s):

wine name:

producer:

region/appellation:

grape varieties:

vintage: alcohol: price:

COLOR DEPTH:
watery | pale | medium | deep | dark

COLOR HUE:
WHITE: greenish | yellow | straw yellow | gold | amber
RED: purplish | ruby | red | garnet | brick | brown
ROSÉ: pink | salmon | orange | copper

CLARITY:
clear | slight haze | cloudy

AROMA INTENSITY:
low | moderate | aromatic | powerful

DEVELOPMENT:
youthful | some age | aged

AROMAS:

DRY/SWEET:
bone dry | dry | off dry | medium sweet | sweet | very sweet

BODY:
very light | light | medium | medium-full | full-bodied | heavy

ACIDITY:
tart | crisp | fresh | smooth | flabby

TANNINS (IF PRESENT):
LEVEL: low | medium | high   TYPE: soft | round | dry | hard

BALANCE:
good | fair | unbalanced (excess: alcohol - acid - tannin - sugar)

FLAVOR INTENSITY:
low | moderate | flavorful | powerful

FLAVORS:

FINISH:
short (< 3 sec) | medium (4-5) | long (5-7) | v. long (>8 sec)

CONCLUSION:

STYLE:
traditional | in-between | modern

rating: ☆ ☆ ☆ ☆ ☆

FOOD: ## FOOD PAIRING:
                    MATCH: perfect | good | neutral | bad

tasting date: location:

tasting partner(s):

wine name:

producer:

region/appellation:

grape varieties:

vintage: alcohol: price:

COLOR DEPTH:
watery | pale | medium | deep | dark

COLOR HUE:
WHITE: greenish | yellow | straw yellow | gold | amber
RED: purplish | ruby | red | garnet | brick | brown
ROSÉ: pink | salmon | orange | copper

CLARITY:
clear | slight haze | cloudy

AROMA INTENSITY:
low | moderate | aromatic | powerful

DEVELOPMENT:
youthful | some age | aged

AROMAS:

DRY/SWEET:
bone dry | dry | off dry | medium sweet | sweet | very sweet

BODY:
very light | light | medium | medium-full | full-bodied | heavy

ACIDITY:
tart | crisp | fresh | smooth | flabby

TANNINS (IF PRESENT):
LEVEL: low | medium | high   TYPE: soft | round | dry | hard

BALANCE:
good | fair | unbalanced (excess: alcohol - acid - tannin - sugar)

FLAVOR INTENSITY:
low | moderate | flavorful | powerful

FLAVORS:

FINISH:
short (< 3 sec) | medium (4-5) | long (5-7) | v. long (>8 sec)

CONCLUSION:

STYLE:
traditional | in-between | modern

rating: ☆ ☆ ☆ ☆ ☆

FOOD: **FOOD PAIRING:**
MATCH: perfect | good | neutral | bad

tasting date: location:

tasting partner(s):

wine name:

producer:

region/appellation:

grape varieties:

vintage: alcohol: price:

COLOR DEPTH:
watery | pale | medium | deep | dark

COLOR HUE:
WHITE: greenish | yellow | straw yellow | gold | amber
RED: purplish | ruby | red | garnet | brick | brown
ROSÉ: pink | salmon | orange | copper

CLARITY:
clear | slight haze | cloudy

AROMA INTENSITY:
low | moderate | aromatic | powerful

DEVELOPMENT:
youthful | some age | aged

AROMAS:

DRY/SWEET:
bone dry | dry | off dry | medium sweet | sweet | very sweet

BODY:
very light | light | medium | medium-full | full-bodied | heavy

ACIDITY:
tart | crisp | fresh | smooth | flabby

TANNINS (IF PRESENT):
LEVEL: low | medium | high   TYPE: soft | round | dry | hard

BALANCE:
good | fair | unbalanced (excess: alcohol - acid   tannin - sugar)

FLAVOR INTENSITY:
low | moderate | flavorful | powerful

FLAVORS:

FINISH:
short (< 3 sec) | medium (4-5) | long (5-7) | v. long (>8 sec)

CONCLUSION:

STYLE:
traditional | in-between | modern

rating: ☆ ☆ ☆ ☆ ☆

FOOD: **FOOD PAIRING:**

MATCH: perfect | good | neutral | bad

tasting date: location:

tasting partner(s):

wine name:

producer:

region/appellation:

grape varieties:

vintage: alcohol: price:

COLOR DEPTH:
watery | pale | medium | deep | dark

COLOR HUE:
WHITE: greenish | yellow | straw yellow | gold | amber
RED: purplish | ruby | red | garnet | brick | brown
ROSÉ: pink | salmon | orange | copper

CLARITY:
clear | slight haze | cloudy

AROMA INTENSITY:
low | moderate | aromatic | powerful

DEVELOPMENT:
youthful | some age | aged

AROMAS:

DRY/SWEET:
bone dry | dry | off dry | medium sweet | sweet | very sweet

BODY:
very light | light | medium | medium-full | full-bodied | heavy

ACIDITY:
tart | crisp | fresh | smooth | flabby

TANNINS (IF PRESENT):
LEVEL: low | medium | high   TYPE: soft | round | dry | hard

BALANCE:
good | fair | unbalanced (excess: alcohol - acid - tannin - sugar)

FLAVOR INTENSITY:
low | moderate | flavorful | powerful

FLAVORS:

FINISH:
short (< 3 sec) | medium (4-5) | long (5-7) | v. long (>8 sec)

CONCLUSION:

STYLE:
traditional | in-between | modern

rating: ☆☆☆☆☆

FOOD: **FOOD PAIRING:**
                    MATCH: perfect | good | neutral | bad

tasting date: location:

tasting partner(s):

wine name:

producer:

region/appellation:

grape varieties:

vintage: alcohol: price:

COLOR DEPTH:
watery | pale | medium | deep | dark

COLOR HUE:
WHITE: greenish | yellow | straw yellow | gold | amber
RED: purplish | ruby | red | garnet | brick | brown
ROSÉ: pink | salmon | orange | copper

CLARITY:
clear | slight haze | cloudy

AROMA INTENSITY:
low | moderate | aromatic | powerful

DEVELOPMENT:
youthful | some age | aged

AROMAS:

DRY/SWEET:
bone dry | dry | off dry | medium sweet | sweet | very sweet

BODY:
very light | light | medium | medium-full | full-bodied | heavy

ACIDITY:
tart | crisp | fresh | smooth | flabby

TANNINS (IF PRESENT):
LEVEL: low | medium | high   TYPE: soft | round | dry | hard

BALANCE:
good | fair | unbalanced (excess: alcohol - acid - tannin - sugar)

FLAVOR INTENSITY:
low | moderate | flavorful | powerful

FLAVORS:

FINISH:
short (< 3 sec) | medium (4-5) | long (5-7) | v. long (>8 sec)

CONCLUSION:

STYLE:
traditional | in-between | modern

rating: ☆ ☆ ☆ ☆ ☆

FOOD: ## FOOD PAIRING:
MATCH: perfect | good | neutral | bad

tasting date: location:

tasting partner(s):

wine name:

producer:

region/appellation:

grape varieties:

vintage: alcohol: price:

COLOR DEPTH:
watery | pale | medium | deep | dark

COLOR HUE:
WHITE: greenish | yellow | straw yellow | gold | amber
RED: purplish | ruby | red | garnet | brick | brown
ROSÉ: pink | salmon | orange | copper

CLARITY:
clear | slight haze | cloudy

AROMA INTENSITY:
low | moderate | aromatic | powerful

DEVELOPMENT:
youthful | some age | aged

AROMAS:

DRY/SWEET:
bone dry | dry | off dry | medium sweet | sweet | very sweet

BODY:
very light | light | medium | medium-full | full-bodied | heavy

ACIDITY:
tart | crisp | fresh | smooth | flabby

TANNINS (IF PRESENT):
LEVEL: low | medium | high   TYPE: soft | round | dry | hard

BALANCE:
good | fair | unbalanced (excess: alcohol - acid - tannin - sugar)

FLAVOR INTENSITY:
low | moderate | flavorful | powerful

FLAVORS:

FINISH:
short (< 3 sec) | medium (4-5) | long (5-7) | v. long (>8 sec)

CONCLUSION:

STYLE:
traditional | in-between | modern

rating: ☆ ☆ ☆ ☆ ☆

FOOD: ## FOOD PAIRING:
MATCH: perfect | good | neutral | bad

tasting date: location:

tasting partner(s):

wine name:

producer:

region/appellation:

grape varieties:

vintage: alcohol: price:

COLOR DEPTH:
watery | pale | medium | deep | dark

COLOR HUE:
WHITE: greenish | yellow | straw yellow | gold | amber
RED: purplish | ruby | red | garnet | brick | brown
ROSÉ: pink | salmon | orange | copper

CLARITY:
clear | slight haze | cloudy

AROMA INTENSITY:
low | moderate | aromatic | powerful

DEVELOPMENT:
youthful | some age | aged

AROMAS:

DRY/SWEET:
bone dry | dry | off dry | medium sweet | sweet | very sweet

BODY:
very light | light | medium | medium-full | full-bodied | heavy

ACIDITY:
tart | crisp | fresh | smooth | flabby

TANNINS (IF PRESENT):
LEVEL: low | medium | high   TYPE: soft | round | dry | hard

BALANCE:
good | fair | unbalanced (excess: alcohol - acid - tannin - sugar)

FLAVOR INTENSITY:
low | moderate | flavorful | powerful

FLAVORS:

FINISH:
short (< 3 sec) | medium (4-5) | long (5-7) | v. long (>8 sec)

CONCLUSION:

STYLE:
traditional | in-between | modern

rating: ☆ ☆ ☆ ☆ ☆

FOOD: **FOOD PAIRING:**

MATCH: perfect | good | neutral | bad

tasting date: location:

tasting partner(s):

wine name:

producer:

region/appellation:

grape varieties:

vintage: alcohol: price:

COLOR DEPTH:
watery | pale | medium | deep | dark

COLOR HUE:
WHITE: greenish | yellow | straw yellow | gold | amber
RED: purplish | ruby | red | garnet | brick | brown
ROSÉ: pink | salmon | orange | copper

CLARITY:
clear | slight haze | cloudy

AROMA INTENSITY:
low | moderate | aromatic | powerful

DEVELOPMENT:
youthful | some age | aged

AROMAS:

DRY/SWEET:
bone dry | dry | off dry | medium sweet | sweet | very sweet

BODY:
very light | light | medium | medium-full | full-bodied | heavy

ACIDITY:
tart | crisp | fresh | smooth | flabby

TANNINS (IF PRESENT):
LEVEL: low | medium | high   TYPE: soft | round | dry | hard

BALANCE:
good | fair | unbalanced (excess: alcohol - acid - tannin - sugar)

FLAVOR INTENSITY:
low | moderate | flavorful | powerful

FLAVORS:

FINISH:
short (< 3 sec) | medium (4-5) | long (5-7) | v. long (>8 sec)

CONCLUSION:

STYLE:
traditional | in-between | modern

rating: ☆ ☆ ☆ ☆ ☆

FOOD: **FOOD PAIRING:**

MATCH: perfect | good | neutral | bad

tasting date: location:

tasting partner(s):

wine name:

producer:

region/appellation:

grape varieties:

vintage: alcohol: price:

COLOR DEPTH:
watery | pale | medium | deep | dark

COLOR HUE:
WHITE: greenish | yellow | straw yellow | gold | amber
RED: purplish | ruby | red | garnet | brick | brown
ROSÉ: pink | salmon | orange | copper

CLARITY:
clear | slight haze | cloudy

AROMA INTENSITY:
low | moderate | aromatic | powerful

DEVELOPMENT:
youthful | some age | aged

AROMAS:

DRY/SWEET:
bone dry | dry | off dry | medium sweet | sweet | very sweet

BODY:
very light | light | medium | medium-full | full-bodied | heavy

ACIDITY:
tart | crisp | fresh | smooth | flabby

TANNINS (IF PRESENT):
LEVEL: low | medium | high   TYPE: soft | round | dry | hard

BALANCE:
good | fair | unbalanced (excess: alcohol - acid - tannin - sugar)

FLAVOR INTENSITY:
low | moderate | flavorful | powerful

FLAVORS:

FINISH:
short (< 3 sec) | medium (4-5) | long (5-7) | v. long (>8 sec)

CONCLUSION:

STYLE:
traditional | in-between | modern

rating: ☆ ☆ ☆ ☆ ☆

FOOD: **FOOD PAIRING:**
                MATCH: perfect | good | neutral | bad

tasting date: location:

tasting partner(s):

wine name:

producer:

region/appellation:

grape varieties:

vintage: alcohol: price:

 COLOR DEPTH:
watery | pale | medium | deep | dark

COLOR HUE:
WHITE: greenish | yellow | straw yellow | gold | amber
RED: purplish | ruby | red | garnet | brick | brown
ROSÉ: pink | salmon | orange | copper

CLARITY:
clear | slight haze | cloudy

 AROMA INTENSITY:
low | moderate | aromatic | powerful

DEVELOPMENT:
youthful | some age | aged

AROMAS:

 DRY/SWEET:
bone dry | dry | off dry | medium sweet | sweet | very sweet

BODY:
very light | light | medium | medium-full | full-bodied | heavy

ACIDITY:
tart | crisp | fresh | smooth | flabby

TANNINS (IF PRESENT):
LEVEL: low | medium | high   TYPE: soft | round | dry | hard

BALANCE:
good | fair | unbalanced (excess: alcohol - acid - tannin - sugar)

FLAVOR INTENSITY:
low | moderate | flavorful | powerful

FLAVORS:

FINISH:
short (< 3 sec) | medium (4-5) | long (5-7) | v. long (>8 sec)

CONCLUSION:

STYLE:
traditional | in-between | modern

rating: ☆☆☆☆☆

FOOD: **FOOD PAIRING:**
MATCH: perfect | good | neutral | bad

tasting date: location:

tasting partner(s):

wine name:

producer:

region/appellation:

grape varieties:

vintage: alcohol: price:

COLOR DEPTH:
watery | pale | medium | deep | dark

COLOR HUE:
WHITE: greenish | yellow | straw yellow | gold | amber
RED: purplish | ruby | red | garnet | brick | brown
ROSÉ: pink | salmon | orange | copper

CLARITY:
clear | slight haze | cloudy

AROMA INTENSITY:
low | moderate | aromatic | powerful

DEVELOPMENT:
youthful | some age | aged

AROMAS:

DRY/SWEET:
bone dry | dry | off dry | medium sweet | sweet | very sweet

BODY:
very light | light | medium | medium-full | full-bodied | heavy

ACIDITY:
tart | crisp | fresh | smooth | flabby

TANNINS (IF PRESENT):
LEVEL: low | medium | high   TYPE: soft | round | dry | hard

BALANCE:
good | fair | unbalanced (excess: alcohol - acid - tannin - sugar)

FLAVOR INTENSITY:
low | moderate | flavorful | powerful

FLAVORS:

FINISH:
short (< 3 sec) | medium (4-5) | long (5-7) | v. long (>8 sec)

CONCLUSION:

STYLE:
traditional | in-between | modern

rating: ☆ ☆ ☆ ☆ ☆

FOOD: **FOOD PAIRING:**

MATCH: perfect | good | neutral | bad

tasting date: location:

tasting partner(s):

wine name:

producer:

region/appellation:

grape varieties:

vintage: alcohol: price:

COLOR DEPTH:
watery | pale | medium | deep | dark

COLOR HUE:
WHITE: greenish | yellow | straw yellow | gold | amber
RED: purplish | ruby | red | garnet | brick | brown
ROSÉ: pink | salmon | orange | copper

CLARITY:
clear | slight haze | cloudy

AROMA INTENSITY:
low | moderate | aromatic | powerful

DEVELOPMENT:
youthful | some age | aged

AROMAS:

DRY/SWEET:
bone dry | dry | off dry | medium sweet | sweet | very sweet

BODY:
very light | light | medium | medium-full | full-bodied | heavy

ACIDITY:
tart | crisp | fresh | smooth | flabby

TANNINS (IF PRESENT):
LEVEL: low | medium | high   TYPE: soft | round | dry | hard

BALANCE:
good | fair | unbalanced (excess: alcohol - acid - tannin - sugar)

FLAVOR INTENSITY:
low | moderate | flavorful | powerful

FLAVORS:

FINISH:
short (< 3 sec) | medium (4-5) | long (5-7) | v. long (>8 sec)

CONCLUSION:

STYLE:
traditional | in-between | modern

rating: ☆ ☆ ☆ ☆ ☆

FOOD: **FOOD PAIRING:**
MATCH: perfect | good | neutral | bad

tasting date: location:

tasting partner(s):

wine name:

producer:

region/appellation:

grape varieties:

vintage: alcohol: price:

COLOR DEPTH:
watery | pale | medium | deep | dark

COLOR HUE:
WHITE: greenish | yellow | straw yellow | gold | amber
RED: purplish | ruby | red | garnet | brick | brown
ROSÉ: pink | salmon | orange | copper

CLARITY:
clear | slight haze | cloudy

AROMA INTENSITY:
low | moderate | aromatic | powerful

DEVELOPMENT:
youthful | some age | aged

AROMAS:

DRY/SWEET:
bone dry | dry | off dry | medium sweet | sweet | very sweet

BODY:
very light | light | medium | medium-full | full-bodied | heavy

ACIDITY:
tart | crisp | fresh | smooth | flabby

TANNINS (IF PRESENT):
LEVEL: low | medium | high   TYPE: soft | round | dry | hard

BALANCE:
good | fair | unbalanced (excess: alcohol - acid - tannin - sugar)

FLAVOR INTENSITY:
low | moderate | flavorful | powerful

FLAVORS:

FINISH:
short (< 3 sec) | medium (4-5) | long (5-7) | v. long (>8 sec)

CONCLUSION:

STYLE:
traditional | in-between | modern

rating: ☆ ☆ ☆ ☆ ☆

FOOD: **FOOD PAIRING:**
MATCH: perfect | good | neutral | bad

tasting date: location:

tasting partner(s):

wine name:

producer:

region/appellation:

grape varieties:

vintage: alcohol: price:

COLOR DEPTH:
watery | pale | medium | deep | dark
COLOR HUE:
WHITE: greenish | yellow | straw yellow | gold | amber
RED: purplish | ruby | red | garnet | brick | brown
ROSÉ: pink | salmon | orange | copper

CLARITY:
clear | slight haze | cloudy

AROMA INTENSITY:
low | moderate | aromatic | powerful
DEVELOPMENT:
youthful | some age | aged
AROMAS:

DRY/SWEET:
bone dry | dry | off dry | medium sweet | sweet | very sweet
BODY:
very light | light | medium | medium-full | full-bodied | heavy
ACIDITY:
tart | crisp | fresh | smooth | flabby
TANNINS (IF PRESENT):
LEVEL: low | medium | high   TYPE: soft | round | dry | hard
BALANCE:
good | fair | unbalanced (excess: alcohol - acid - tannin - sugar)
FLAVOR INTENSITY:
low | moderate | flavorful | powerful
FLAVORS:

FINISH:
short (< 3 sec) | medium (4-5) | long (5-7) | v. long (>8 sec)

CONCLUSION:

STYLE:
traditional | in-between | modern

rating: ☆ ☆ ☆ ☆ ☆

FOOD: **FOOD PAIRING:**
                  MATCH: perfect | good | neutral | bad

tasting date: location:

tasting partner(s):

wine name:

producer:

region/appellation:

grape varieties:

vintage: alcohol: price:

COLOR DEPTH:
watery | pale | medium | deep | dark

COLOR HUE:
WHITE: greenish | yellow | straw yellow | gold | amber
RED: purplish | ruby | red | garnet | brick | brown
ROSÉ: pink | salmon | orange | copper

CLARITY:
clear | slight haze | cloudy

AROMA INTENSITY:
low | moderate | aromatic | powerful

DEVELOPMENT:
youthful | some age | aged

AROMAS:

DRY/SWEET:
bone dry | dry | off dry | medium sweet | sweet | very sweet

BODY:
very light | light | medium | medium-full | full-bodied | heavy

ACIDITY:
tart | crisp | fresh | smooth | flabby

TANNINS (IF PRESENT):
LEVEL: low | medium | high   TYPE: soft | round | dry | hard

BALANCE:
good | fair | unbalanced (excess: alcohol - acid - tannin - sugar)

FLAVOR INTENSITY:
low | moderate | flavorful | powerful

FLAVORS:

FINISH:
short (< 3 sec) | medium (4-5) | long (5-7) | v. long (>8 sec)

CONCLUSION:

STYLE:
traditional | in-between | modern

rating: ☆ ☆ ☆ ☆ ☆

FOOD: **FOOD PAIRING:**
              MATCH: perfect | good | neutral | bad

tasting date: location:

tasting partner(s):

wine name:

producer:

region/appellation:

grape varieties:

vintage: alcohol: price:

COLOR DEPTH:
watery | pale | medium | deep | dark

COLOR HUE:
WHITE: greenish | yellow | straw yellow | gold | amber
RED: purplish | ruby | red | garnet | brick | brown
ROSÉ: pink | salmon | orange | copper

CLARITY:
clear | slight haze | cloudy

AROMA INTENSITY:
low | moderate | aromatic | powerful

DEVELOPMENT:
youthful | some age | aged

AROMAS:

DRY/SWEET:
bone dry | dry | off dry | medium sweet | sweet | very sweet

BODY:
very light | light | medium | medium-full | full-bodied | heavy

ACIDITY:
tart | crisp | fresh | smooth | flabby

TANNINS (IF PRESENT):
LEVEL: low | medium | high   TYPE: soft | round | dry | hard

BALANCE:
good | fair | unbalanced (excess: alcohol - acid - tannin - sugar)

FLAVOR INTENSITY:
low | moderate | flavorful | powerful

FLAVORS:

FINISH:
short (< 3 sec) | medium (4-5) | long (5-7) | v. long (>8 sec)

CONCLUSION:

STYLE:
traditional | in-between | modern

rating: ☆ ☆ ☆ ☆ ☆

FOOD: **FOOD PAIRING:**
                MATCH: perfect | good | neutral | bad

tasting date: location:

tasting partner(s):

wine name:

producer:

region/appellation:

grape varieties:

vintage: alcohol: price:

COLOR DEPTH:
watery | pale | medium | deep | dark

COLOR HUE:
WHITE: greenish | yellow | straw yellow | gold | amber
RED: purplish | ruby | red | garnet | brick | brown
ROSÉ: pink | salmon | orange | copper

CLARITY:
clear | slight haze | cloudy

AROMA INTENSITY:
low | moderate | aromatic | powerful

DEVELOPMENT:
youthful | some age | aged

AROMAS:

DRY/SWEET:
bone dry | dry | off dry | medium sweet | sweet | very sweet

BODY:
very light | light | medium | medium-full | full-bodied | heavy

ACIDITY:
tart | crisp | fresh | smooth | flabby

TANNINS (IF PRESENT):
LEVEL: low | medium | high   TYPE: soft | round | dry | hard

BALANCE:
good | fair | unbalanced (excess: alcohol - acid - tannin - sugar)

FLAVOR INTENSITY:
low | moderate | flavorful | powerful

FLAVORS:

FINISH:
short (< 3 sec) | medium (4-5) | long (5-7) | v. long (>8 sec)

CONCLUSION:

STYLE:
traditional | in-between | modern

rating: ☆ ☆ ☆ ☆ ☆

FOOD: **FOOD PAIRING:**
                   MATCH: perfect | good | neutral | bad

tasting date: location:

tasting partner(s):

wine name:

producer:

region/appellation:

grape varieties:

vintage: alcohol: price:

COLOR DEPTH:
watery | pale | medium | deep | dark

COLOR HUE:
WHITE: greenish | yellow | straw yellow | gold | amber
RED: purplish | ruby | red | garnet | brick | brown
ROSÉ: pink | salmon | orange | copper

CLARITY:
clear | slight haze | cloudy

AROMA INTENSITY:
low | moderate | aromatic | powerful

DEVELOPMENT:
youthful | some age | aged

AROMAS:

DRY/SWEET:
bone dry | dry | off dry | medium sweet | sweet | very sweet

BODY:
very light | light | medium | medium-full | full-bodied | heavy

ACIDITY:
tart | crisp | fresh | smooth | flabby

TANNINS (IF PRESENT):
LEVEL: low | medium | high   TYPE: soft | round | dry | hard

BALANCE:
good | fair | unbalanced (excess: alcohol - acid - tannin - sugar)

FLAVOR INTENSITY:
low | moderate | flavorful | powerful

FLAVORS:

FINISH:
short (< 3 sec) | medium (4-5) | long (5-7) | v. long (>8 sec)

CONCLUSION:

STYLE:
traditional | in-between | modern

rating: ☆ ☆ ☆ ☆ ☆

FOOD: **FOOD PAIRING:**

MATCH: perfect | good | neutral | bad

tasting date: location:

tasting partner(s):

wine name:

producer:

region/appellation:

grape varieties:

vintage: alcohol: price:

COLOR DEPTH:
watery | pale | medium | deep | dark

COLOR HUE:
WHITE: greenish | yellow | straw yellow | gold | amber
RED: purplish | ruby | red | garnet | brick | brown
ROSÉ: pink | salmon | orange | copper

CLARITY:
clear | slight haze | cloudy

AROMA INTENSITY:
low | moderate | aromatic | powerful

DEVELOPMENT:
youthful | some age | aged

AROMAS:

DRY/SWEET:
bone dry | dry | off dry | medium sweet | sweet | very sweet

BODY:
very light | light | medium | medium-full | full-bodied | heavy

ACIDITY:
tart | crisp | fresh | smooth | flabby

TANNINS (IF PRESENT):
LEVEL: low | medium | high   TYPE: soft | round | dry | hard

BALANCE:
good | fair | unbalanced (excess: alcohol - acid - tannin - sugar)

FLAVOR INTENSITY:
low | moderate | flavorful | powerful

FLAVORS:

FINISH:
short (< 3 sec) | medium (4-5) | long (5-7) | v. long (>8 sec)

CONCLUSION:

STYLE:
traditional | in-between | modern

rating: ☆ ☆ ☆ ☆ ☆

FOOD: **FOOD PAIRING:**

MATCH: perfect | good | neutral | bad

tasting date: location:

tasting partner(s):

wine name:

producer:

region/appellation:

grape varieties:

vintage: alcohol: price:

 COLOR DEPTH:
watery | pale | medium | deep | dark

COLOR HUE:
WHITE: greenish | yellow | straw yellow | gold | amber
RED: purplish | ruby | red | garnet | brick | brown
ROSÉ: pink | salmon | orange | copper

CLARITY:
clear | slight haze | cloudy

 AROMA INTENSITY:
low | moderate | aromatic | powerful

DEVELOPMENT:
youthful | some age | aged

AROMAS:

 DRY/SWEET:
bone dry | dry | off dry | medium sweet | sweet | very sweet

BODY:
very light | light | medium | medium-full | full-bodied | heavy

ACIDITY:
tart | crisp | fresh | smooth | flabby

TANNINS (IF PRESENT):
LEVEL: low | medium | high   TYPE: soft | round | dry | hard

BALANCE:
good | fair | unbalanced (excess: alcohol - acid - tannin - sugar)

FLAVOR INTENSITY:
low | moderate | flavorful | powerful

FLAVORS:

FINISH:
short (< 3 sec) | medium (4-5) | long (5-7) | v. long (>8 sec)

CONCLUSION:

STYLE:
traditional | in-between | modern

rating: ☆ ☆ ☆ ☆ ☆

FOOD: **FOOD PAIRING:**
MATCH: perfect | good | neutral | bad

tasting date: location:

tasting partner(s):

wine name:

producer:

region/appellation:

grape varieties:

vintage: alcohol: price:

COLOR DEPTH:
watery | pale | medium | deep | dark

COLOR HUE:
WHITE: greenish | yellow | straw yellow | gold | amber
RED: purplish | ruby | red | garnet | brick | brown
ROSÉ: pink | salmon | orange | copper

CLARITY:
clear | slight haze | cloudy

AROMA INTENSITY:
low | moderate | aromatic | powerful

DEVELOPMENT:
youthful | some age | aged

AROMAS:

DRY/SWEET:
bone dry | dry | off dry | medium sweet | sweet | very sweet

BODY:
very light | light | medium | medium-full | full-bodied | heavy

ACIDITY:
tart | crisp | fresh | smooth | flabby

TANNINS (IF PRESENT):
LEVEL: low | medium | high   TYPE: soft | round | dry | hard

BALANCE:
good | fair | unbalanced (excess: alcohol - acid - tannin - sugar)

FLAVOR INTENSITY:
low | moderate | flavorful | powerful

FLAVORS:

FINISH:
short (< 3 sec) | medium (4-5) | long (5-7) | v. long (>8 sec)

CONCLUSION:

STYLE:
traditional | in-between | modern

rating: ☆ ☆ ☆ ☆ ☆

FOOD: **FOOD PAIRING:**
                  MATCH: perfect | good | neutral | bad

tasting date: location:

tasting partner(s):

wine name:

producer:

region/appellation:

grape varieties:

vintage: alcohol: price:

COLOR DEPTH:
watery | pale | medium | deep | dark

COLOR HUE:
WHITE: greenish | yellow | straw yellow | gold | amber
RED: purplish | ruby | red | garnet | brick | brown
ROSÉ: pink | salmon | orange | copper

CLARITY:
clear | slight haze | cloudy

AROMA INTENSITY:
low | moderate | aromatic | powerful

DEVELOPMENT:
youthful | some age | aged

AROMAS:

DRY/SWEET:
bone dry | dry | off dry | medium sweet | sweet | very sweet

BODY:
very light | light | medium | medium-full | full-bodied | heavy

ACIDITY:
tart | crisp | fresh | smooth | flabby

TANNINS (IF PRESENT):
LEVEL: low | medium | high   TYPE: soft | round | dry | hard

BALANCE:
good | fair | unbalanced (excess: alcohol - acid - tannin - sugar)

FLAVOR INTENSITY:
low | moderate | flavorful | powerful

FLAVORS:

FINISH:
short (< 3 sec) | medium (4-5) | long (5-7) | v. long (>8 sec)

CONCLUSION:

STYLE:
traditional | in-between | modern

rating: ☆ ☆ ☆ ☆ ☆

FOOD: **FOOD PAIRING:**

MATCH: perfect | good | neutral | bad

tasting date: location:

tasting partner(s):

wine name:

producer:

region/appellation:

grape varieties:

vintage: alcohol: price:

COLOR DEPTH:
watery | pale | medium | deep | dark

COLOR HUE:
WHITE: greenish | yellow | straw yellow | gold | amber
RED: purplish | ruby | red | garnet | brick | brown
ROSÉ: pink | salmon | orange | copper

CLARITY:
clear | slight haze | cloudy

AROMA INTENSITY:
low | moderate | aromatic | powerful

DEVELOPMENT:
youthful | some age | aged

AROMAS:

DRY/SWEET:
bone dry | dry | off dry | medium sweet | sweet | very sweet

BODY:
very light | light | medium | medium-full | full-bodied | heavy

ACIDITY:
tart | crisp | fresh | smooth | flabby

TANNINS (IF PRESENT):
LEVEL: low | medium | high   TYPE: soft | round | dry | hard

BALANCE:
good | fair | unbalanced (excess: alcohol - acid - tannin - sugar)

FLAVOR INTENSITY:
low | moderate | flavorful | powerful

FLAVORS:

FINISH:
short (< 3 sec) | medium (4-5) | long (5-7) | v. long (>8 sec)

CONCLUSION:

STYLE:
traditional | in-between | modern

rating: ☆ ☆ ☆ ☆ ☆

FOOD: **FOOD PAIRING:**
                    MATCH: perfect | good | neutral | bad

tasting date: location:

tasting partner(s):

wine name:

producer:

region/appellation:

grape varieties:

vintage: alcohol: price:

 COLOR DEPTH:
watery | pale | medium | deep | dark

COLOR HUE:
WHITE: greenish | yellow | straw yellow | gold | amber
RED: purplish | ruby | red | garnet | brick | brown
ROSÉ: pink | salmon | orange | copper

CLARITY:
clear | slight haze | cloudy

 AROMA INTENSITY:
low | moderate | aromatic | powerful

DEVELOPMENT:
youthful | some age | aged

AROMAS:

 DRY/SWEET:
bone dry | dry | off dry | medium sweet | sweet | very sweet

BODY:
very light | light | medium | medium-full | full-bodied | heavy

ACIDITY:
tart | crisp | fresh | smooth | flabby

TANNINS (IF PRESENT):
LEVEL: low | medium | high   TYPE: soft | round | dry | hard

BALANCE:
good | fair | unbalanced (excess: alcohol - acid - tannin - sugar)

FLAVOR INTENSITY:
low | moderate | flavorful | powerful

FLAVORS:

FINISH:
short (< 3 sec) | medium (4-5) | long (5-7) | v. long (>8 sec)

CONCLUSION:

STYLE:
traditional | in-between | modern

rating: ☆ ☆ ☆ ☆ ☆

FOOD: **FOOD PAIRING:**
                  MATCH: perfect | good | neutral | bad

tasting date: location:

tasting partner(s):

wine name:

producer:

region/appellation:

grape varieties:

vintage: alcohol: price:

COLOR DEPTH:
watery | pale | medium | deep | dark

COLOR HUE:
WHITE: greenish | yellow | straw yellow | gold | amber
RED: purplish | ruby | red | garnet | brick | brown
ROSÉ: pink | salmon | orange | copper

CLARITY:
clear | slight haze | cloudy

AROMA INTENSITY:
low | moderate | aromatic | powerful

DEVELOPMENT:
youthful | some age | aged

AROMAS:

DRY/SWEET:
bone dry | dry | off dry | medium sweet | sweet | very sweet

BODY:
very light | light | medium | medium-full | full-bodied | heavy

ACIDITY:
tart | crisp | fresh | smooth | flabby

TANNINS (IF PRESENT):
LEVEL: low | medium | high   TYPE: soft | round | dry | hard

BALANCE:
good | fair | unbalanced (excess: alcohol - acid - tannin - sugar)

FLAVOR INTENSITY:
low | moderate | flavorful | powerful

FLAVORS:

FINISH:
short (< 3 sec) | medium (4-5) | long (5-7) | v. long (>8 sec)

CONCLUSION:

STYLE:
traditional | in-between | modern

rating: ☆ ☆ ☆ ☆ ☆

FOOD: **FOOD PAIRING:**
                   MATCH: perfect | good | neutral | bad

tasting date: location:

tasting partner(s):

wine name:

producer:

region/appellation:

grape varieties:

vintage: alcohol: price:

COLOR DEPTH:
watery | pale | medium | deep | dark

COLOR HUE:
WHITE: greenish | yellow | straw yellow | gold | amber
RED: purplish | ruby | red | garnet | brick | brown
ROSÉ: pink | salmon | orange | copper

CLARITY:
clear | slight haze | cloudy

AROMA INTENSITY:
low | moderate | aromatic | powerful

DEVELOPMENT:
youthful | some age | aged

AROMAS:

DRY/SWEET:
bone dry | dry | off dry | medium sweet | sweet | very sweet

BODY:
very light | light | medium | medium-full | full-bodied | heavy

ACIDITY:
tart | crisp | fresh | smooth | flabby

TANNINS (IF PRESENT):
LEVEL: low | medium | high TYPE: soft | round | dry | hard

BALANCE:
good | fair | unbalanced (excess: alcohol - acid - tannin - sugar)

FLAVOR INTENSITY:
low | moderate | flavorful | powerful

FLAVORS:

FINISH:
short (< 3 sec) | medium (4-5) | long (5-7) | v. long (>8 sec)

CONCLUSION:

STYLE:
traditional | in-between | modern

rating: ☆☆☆☆☆

FOOD: ### FOOD PAIRING:
MATCH: perfect | good | neutral | bad

tasting date: location:

tasting partner(s):

wine name:

producer:

region/appellation:

grape varieties:

vintage: alcohol: price:

COLOR DEPTH:
watery | pale | medium | deep | dark

COLOR HUE:
WHITE: greenish | yellow | straw yellow | gold | amber
RED: purplish | ruby | red | garnet | brick | brown
ROSÉ: pink | salmon | orange | copper

CLARITY:
clear | slight haze | cloudy

AROMA INTENSITY:
low | moderate | aromatic | powerful

DEVELOPMENT:
youthful | some age | aged

AROMAS:

DRY/SWEET:
bone dry | dry | off dry | medium sweet | sweet | very sweet

BODY:
very light | light | medium | medium-full | full-bodied | heavy

ACIDITY:
tart | crisp | fresh | smooth | flabby

TANNINS (IF PRESENT):
LEVEL: low | medium | high   TYPE: soft | round | dry | hard

BALANCE:
good | fair | unbalanced (excess: alcohol - acid - tannin - sugar)

FLAVOR INTENSITY:
low | moderate | flavorful | powerful

FLAVORS:

FINISH:
short (< 3 sec) | medium (4-5) | long (5-7) | v. long (>8 sec)

CONCLUSION:

STYLE:
traditional | in-between | modern

rating: ☆ ☆ ☆ ☆ ☆

FOOD: **FOOD PAIRING:**
                 MATCH: perfect | good | neutral | bad

tasting date: location:

tasting partner(s):

wine name:

producer:

region/appellation:

grape varieties:

vintage: alcohol: price:

COLOR DEPTH:
watery | pale | medium | deep | dark
COLOR HUE:
WHITE: greenish | yellow | straw yellow | gold | amber
RED: purplish | ruby | red | garnet | brick | brown
ROSÉ: pink | salmon | orange | copper

CLARITY:
clear | slight haze | cloudy

AROMA INTENSITY:
low | moderate | aromatic | powerful
DEVELOPMENT:
youthful | some age | aged
AROMAS:

DRY/SWEET:
bone dry | dry | off dry | medium sweet | sweet | very sweet
BODY:
very light | light | medium | medium-full | full-bodied | heavy
ACIDITY:
tart | crisp | fresh | smooth | flabby
TANNINS (IF PRESENT):
LEVEL: low | medium | high   TYPE: soft | round | dry | hard
BALANCE:
good | fair | unbalanced (excess: alcohol - acid - tannin - sugar)
FLAVOR INTENSITY:
low | moderate | flavorful | powerful
FLAVORS:

FINISH:
short (< 3 sec) | medium (4-5) | long (5-7) | v. long (>8 sec)
CONCLUSION:

STYLE:
traditional | in-between | modern
rating: ☆☆☆☆☆

FOOD: ### FOOD PAIRING:
MATCH: perfect | good | neutral | bad

tasting date: location:

tasting partner(s):

wine name:

producer:

region/appellation:

grape varieties:

vintage: alcohol: price:

COLOR DEPTH:
watery | pale | medium | deep | dark
COLOR HUE:
WHITE: greenish | yellow | straw yellow | gold | amber
RED: purplish | ruby | red | garnet | brick | brown
ROSÉ: pink | salmon | orange | copper
CLARITY:
clear | slight haze | cloudy

AROMA INTENSITY:
low | moderate | aromatic | powerful
DEVELOPMENT:
youthful | some age | aged
AROMAS:

DRY/SWEET:
bone dry | dry | off dry | medium sweet | sweet | very sweet
BODY:
very light | light | medium | medium-full | full-bodied | heavy
ACIDITY:
tart | crisp | fresh | smooth | flabby
TANNINS (IF PRESENT):
LEVEL: low | medium | high TYPE: soft | round | dry | hard
BALANCE:
good | fair | unbalanced (excess: alcohol - acid - tannin - sugar)
FLAVOR INTENSITY:
low | moderate | flavorful | powerful
FLAVORS:

FINISH:
short (< 3 sec) | medium (4-5) | long (5-7) | v. long (>8 sec)
CONCLUSION:

STYLE:
traditional | in-between | modern
rating: ☆ ☆ ☆ ☆ ☆

FOOD: **FOOD PAIRING:**
MATCH: perfect | good | neutral | bad

tasting date: location:

tasting partner(s):

wine name:

producer:

region/appellation:

grape varieties:

vintage: alcohol: price:

COLOR DEPTH:
watery | pale | medium | deep | dark

COLOR HUE:
WHITE: greenish | yellow | straw yellow | gold | amber
RED: purplish | ruby | red | garnet | brick | brown
ROSÉ: pink | salmon | orange | copper

CLARITY:
clear | slight haze | cloudy

AROMA INTENSITY:
low | moderate | aromatic | powerful

DEVELOPMENT:
youthful | some age | aged

AROMAS:

DRY/SWEET:
bone dry | dry | off dry | medium sweet | sweet | very sweet

BODY:
very light | light | medium | medium-full | full-bodied | heavy

ACIDITY:
tart | crisp | fresh | smooth | flabby

TANNINS (IF PRESENT):
LEVEL: low | medium | high   TYPE: soft | round | dry | hard

BALANCE:
good | fair | unbalanced (excess: alcohol - acid - tannin - sugar)

FLAVOR INTENSITY:
low | moderate | flavorful | powerful

FLAVORS:

FINISH:
short (< 3 sec) | medium (4-5) | long (5-7) | v. long (>8 sec)

CONCLUSION:

STYLE:
traditional | in-between | modern

rating: ☆ ☆ ☆ ☆ ☆

FOOD: ## FOOD PAIRING:
MATCH: perfect | good | neutral | bad

tasting date: location:

tasting partner(s):

wine name:

producer:

region/appellation:

grape varieties:

vintage: alcohol: price:

COLOR DEPTH:
watery | pale | medium | deep | dark

COLOR HUE:
WHITE: greenish | yellow | straw yellow | gold | amber
RED: purplish | ruby | red | garnet | brick | brown
ROSÉ: pink | salmon | orange | copper

CLARITY:
clear | slight haze | cloudy

AROMA INTENSITY:
low | moderate | aromatic | powerful

DEVELOPMENT:
youthful | some age | aged

AROMAS:

DRY/SWEET:
bone dry | dry | off dry | medium sweet | sweet | very sweet

BODY:
very light | light | medium | medium-full | full-bodied | heavy

ACIDITY:
tart | crisp | fresh | smooth | flabby

TANNINS (IF PRESENT):
LEVEL: low | medium | high   TYPE: soft | round | dry | hard

BALANCE:
good | fair | unbalanced (excess: alcohol - acid - tannin - sugar)

FLAVOR INTENSITY:
low | moderate | flavorful | powerful

FLAVORS:

FINISH:
short (< 3 sec) | medium (4-5) | long (5-7) | v. long (>8 sec)

CONCLUSION:

STYLE:
traditional | in-between | modern

rating: ☆ ☆ ☆ ☆ ☆

FOOD: **FOOD PAIRING:**
MATCH: perfect | good | neutral | bad

tasting date: location:

tasting partner(s):

wine name:

producer:

region/appellation:

grape varieties:

vintage: alcohol: price:

COLOR DEPTH:
watery | pale | medium | deep | dark

COLOR HUE:
WHITE: greenish | yellow | straw yellow | gold | amber
RED: purplish | ruby | red | garnet | brick | brown
ROSÉ: pink | salmon | orange | copper

CLARITY:
clear | slight haze | cloudy

AROMA INTENSITY:
low | moderate | aromatic | powerful

DEVELOPMENT:
youthful | some age | aged

AROMAS:

DRY/SWEET:
bone dry | dry | off dry | medium sweet | sweet | very sweet

BODY:
very light | light | medium | medium-full | full-bodied | heavy

ACIDITY:
tart | crisp | fresh | smooth | flabby

TANNINS (IF PRESENT):
LEVEL: low | medium | high   **TYPE:** soft | round | dry | hard

BALANCE:
good | fair | unbalanced (excess: alcohol - acid - tannin - sugar)

FLAVOR INTENSITY:
low | moderate | flavorful | powerful

FLAVORS:

FINISH:
short (< 3 sec) | medium (4-5) | long (5-7) | v. long (>8 sec)

CONCLUSION:

STYLE:
traditional | in-between | modern

rating: ☆ ☆ ☆ ☆ ☆

FOOD: **FOOD PAIRING:**

MATCH: perfect | good | neutral | bad

tasting date: location:

tasting partner(s):

wine name:

producer:

region/appellation:

grape varieties:

vintage: alcohol: price:

COLOR DEPTH:
watery | pale | medium | deep | dark

COLOR HUE:
WHITE: greenish | yellow | straw yellow | gold | amber
RED: purplish | ruby | red | garnet | brick | brown
ROSÉ: pink | salmon | orange | copper

CLARITY:
clear | slight haze | cloudy

AROMA INTENSITY:
low | moderate | aromatic | powerful

DEVELOPMENT:
youthful | some age | aged

AROMAS:

DRY/SWEET:
bone dry | dry | off dry | medium sweet | sweet | very sweet

BODY:
very light | light | medium | medium-full | full-bodied | heavy

ACIDITY:
tart | crisp | fresh | smooth | flabby

TANNINS (IF PRESENT):
LEVEL: low | medium | high   TYPE: soft | round | dry | hard

BALANCE:
good | fair | unbalanced (excess: alcohol - acid - tannin - sugar)

FLAVOR INTENSITY:
low | moderate | flavorful | powerful

FLAVORS:

FINISH:
short (< 3 sec) | medium (4-5) | long (5-7) | v. long (>8 sec)

CONCLUSION:

STYLE:
traditional | in-between | modern

rating: ☆ ☆ ☆ ☆ ☆

FOOD: **FOOD PAIRING:**

MATCH: perfect | good | neutral | bad

tasting date: location:

tasting partner(s):

wine name:

producer:

region/appellation:

grape varieties:

vintage: alcohol: price:

COLOR DEPTH:
watery | pale | medium | deep | dark

COLOR HUE:
WHITE: greenish | yellow | straw yellow | gold | amber
RED: purplish | ruby | red | garnet | brick | brown
ROSÉ: pink | salmon | orange | copper

CLARITY:
clear | slight haze | cloudy

AROMA INTENSITY:
low | moderate | aromatic | powerful

DEVELOPMENT:
youthful | some age | aged

AROMAS:

DRY/SWEET:
bone dry | dry | off dry | medium sweet | sweet | very sweet

BODY:
very light | light | medium | medium-full | full-bodied | heavy

ACIDITY:
tart | crisp | fresh | smooth | flabby

TANNINS (IF PRESENT):
LEVEL: low | medium | high   TYPE: soft | round | dry | hard

BALANCE:
good | fair | unbalanced (excess: alcohol - acid - tannin - sugar)

FLAVOR INTENSITY:
low | moderate | flavorful | powerful

FLAVORS:

FINISH:
short (< 3 sec) | medium (4-5) | long (5-7) | v. long (>8 sec)

CONCLUSION:

STYLE:
traditional | in-between | modern

rating: ☆ ☆ ☆ ☆ ☆

FOOD: **FOOD PAIRING:**

MATCH: perfect | good | neutral | bad

tasting date: location:

tasting partner(s):

wine name:

producer:

region/appellation:

grape varieties:

vintage: alcohol: price:

COLOR DEPTH:
watery | pale | medium | deep | dark

COLOR HUE:
WHITE: greenish | yellow | straw yellow | gold | amber
RED: purplish | ruby | red | garnet | brick | brown
ROSÉ: pink | salmon | orange | copper

CLARITY:
clear | slight haze | cloudy

AROMA INTENSITY:
low | moderate | aromatic | powerful

DEVELOPMENT:
youthful | some age | aged

AROMAS:

DRY/SWEET:
bone dry | dry | off dry | medium sweet | sweet | very sweet

BODY:
very light | light | medium | medium-full | full-bodied | heavy

ACIDITY:
tart | crisp | fresh | smooth | flabby

TANNINS (IF PRESENT):
LEVEL: low | medium | high   TYPE: soft | round | dry | hard

BALANCE:
good | fair | unbalanced (excess: alcohol - acid - tannin - sugar)

FLAVOR INTENSITY:
low | moderate | flavorful | powerful

FLAVORS:

FINISH:
short (< 3 sec) | medium (4-5) | long (5-7) | v. long (>8 sec)

CONCLUSION:

STYLE:
traditional | in-between | modern

rating: ☆ ☆ ☆ ☆ ☆

FOOD: **FOOD PAIRING:**

                                MATCH: perfect | good | neutral | bad

tasting date: location:

tasting partner(s):

wine name:

producer:

region/appellation:

grape varieties:

vintage: alcohol: price:

COLOR DEPTH:
watery | pale | medium | deep | dark
COLOR HUE:
WHITE: greenish | yellow | straw yellow | gold | amber
RED: purplish | ruby | red | garnet | brick | brown
ROSÉ: pink | salmon | orange | copper

CLARITY:
clear | slight haze | cloudy

AROMA INTENSITY:
low | moderate | aromatic | powerful
DEVELOPMENT:
youthful | some age | aged
AROMAS:

DRY/SWEET:
bone dry | dry | off dry | medium sweet | sweet | very sweet
BODY:
very light | light | medium | medium-full | full-bodied | heavy
ACIDITY:
tart | crisp | fresh | smooth | flabby
TANNINS (IF PRESENT):
LEVEL: low | medium | high   TYPE: soft | round | dry | hard
BALANCE:
good | fair | unbalanced (excess: alcohol - acid - tannin - sugar)
FLAVOR INTENSITY:
low | moderate | flavorful | powerful
FLAVORS:

FINISH:
short (< 3 sec) | medium (4-5) | long (5-7) | v. long (>8 sec)

CONCLUSION:

STYLE:
traditional | in-between | modern

rating: ☆ ☆ ☆ ☆ ☆

FOOD: **FOOD PAIRING:**
                   MATCH: perfect | good | neutral | bad

tasting date: location:

tasting partner(s):

wine name:

producer:

region/appellation:

grape varieties:

vintage: alcohol: price:

COLOR DEPTH:
watery | pale | medium | deep | dark

COLOR HUE:
WHITE: greenish | yellow | straw yellow | gold | amber
RED: purplish | ruby | red | garnet | brick | brown
ROSÉ: pink | salmon | orange | copper

CLARITY:
clear | slight haze | cloudy

AROMA INTENSITY:
low | moderate | aromatic | powerful

DEVELOPMENT:
youthful | some age | aged

AROMAS:

DRY/SWEET:
bone dry | dry | off dry | medium sweet | sweet | very sweet

BODY:
very light | light | medium | medium-full | full-bodied | heavy

ACIDITY:
tart | crisp | fresh | smooth | flabby

TANNINS (IF PRESENT):
LEVEL: low | medium | high   TYPE: soft | round | dry | hard

BALANCE:
good | fair | unbalanced (excess: alcohol - acid - tannin - sugar)

FLAVOR INTENSITY:
low | moderate | flavorful | powerful

FLAVORS:

FINISH:
short (< 3 sec) | medium (4-5) | long (5-7) | v. long (>8 sec)

CONCLUSION:

STYLE:
traditional | in-between | modern

rating: ☆ ☆ ☆ ☆ ☆

FOOD: **FOOD PAIRING:**
                    MATCH: perfect | good | neutral | bad

tasting date: location:

tasting partner(s):

wine name:

producer:

region/appellation:

grape varieties:

vintage: alcohol: price:

COLOR DEPTH:
watery | pale | medium | deep | dark

COLOR HUE:
WHITE: greenish | yellow | straw yellow | gold | amber
RED: purplish | ruby | red | garnet | brick | brown
ROSÉ: pink | salmon | orange | copper

CLARITY:
clear | slight haze | cloudy

AROMA INTENSITY:
low | moderate | aromatic | powerful

DEVELOPMENT:
youthful | some age | aged

AROMAS:

DRY/SWEET:
bone dry | dry | off dry | medium sweet | sweet | very sweet

BODY:
very light | light | medium | medium-full | full-bodied | heavy

ACIDITY:
tart | crisp | fresh | smooth | flabby

TANNINS (IF PRESENT):
LEVEL: low | medium | high   TYPE: soft | round | dry | hard

BALANCE:
good | fair | unbalanced (excess: alcohol - acid - tannin - sugar)

FLAVOR INTENSITY:
low | moderate | flavorful | powerful

FLAVORS:

FINISH:
short (< 3 sec) | medium (4-5) | long (5-7) | v. long (>8 sec)

CONCLUSION:

STYLE:
traditional | in-between | modern

rating: ☆ ☆ ☆ ☆ ☆

FOOD: **FOOD PAIRING:**
                        MATCH: perfect | good | neutral | bad

tasting date: location:

tasting partner(s):

wine name:

producer:

region/appellation:

grape varieties:

vintage: alcohol: price:

COLOR DEPTH:
watery | pale | medium | deep | dark

COLOR HUE:
WHITE: greenish | yellow | straw yellow | gold | amber
RED: purplish | ruby | red | garnet | brick | brown
ROSÉ: pink | salmon | orange | copper

CLARITY:
clear | slight haze | cloudy

AROMA INTENSITY:
low | moderate | aromatic | powerful

DEVELOPMENT:
youthful | some age | aged

AROMAS:

DRY/SWEET:
bone dry | dry | off dry | medium sweet | sweet | very sweet

BODY:
very light | light | medium | medium-full | full-bodied | heavy

ACIDITY:
tart | crisp | fresh | smooth | flabby

TANNINS (IF PRESENT):
LEVEL: low | medium | high   TYPE: soft | round | dry | hard

BALANCE:
good | fair | unbalanced (excess: alcohol - acid - tannin - sugar)

FLAVOR INTENSITY:
low | moderate | flavorful | powerful

FLAVORS:

FINISH:
short (< 3 sec) | medium (4-5) | long (5-7) | v. long (>8 sec)

CONCLUSION:

STYLE:
traditional | in-between | modern

rating: ☆ ☆ ☆ ☆ ☆

FOOD: ### FOOD PAIRING:
MATCH: perfect | good | neutral | bad

tasting date: location:

tasting partner(s):

wine name:

producer:

region/appellation:

grape varieties:

vintage: alcohol: price:

COLOR DEPTH:
watery | pale | medium | deep | dark

COLOR HUE:
WHITE: greenish | yellow | straw yellow | gold | amber
RED: purplish | ruby | red | garnet | brick | brown
ROSÉ: pink | salmon | orange | copper

CLARITY:
clear | slight haze | cloudy

AROMA INTENSITY:
low | moderate | aromatic | powerful

DEVELOPMENT:
youthful | some age | aged

AROMAS:

DRY/SWEET:
bone dry | dry | off dry | medium sweet | sweet | very sweet

BODY:
very light | light | medium | medium-full | full-bodied | heavy

ACIDITY:
tart | crisp | fresh | smooth | flabby

TANNINS (IF PRESENT):
LEVEL: low | medium | high   TYPE: soft | round | dry | hard

BALANCE:
good | fair | unbalanced (excess: alcohol - acid - tannin - sugar)

FLAVOR INTENSITY:
low | moderate | flavorful | powerful

FLAVORS:

FINISH:
short (< 3 sec) | medium (4-5) | long (5-7) | v. long (>8 sec)

CONCLUSION:

STYLE:
traditional | in-between | modern

rating: ☆ ☆ ☆ ☆ ☆

FOOD: **FOOD PAIRING:**

MATCH: perfect | good | neutral | bad

tasting date: location:

tasting partner(s):

wine name:

producer:

region/appellation:

grape varieties:

vintage: alcohol: price:

COLOR DEPTH:
watery | pale | medium | deep | dark

COLOR HUE:
WHITE: greenish | yellow | straw yellow | gold | amber
RED: purplish | ruby | red | garnet | brick | brown
ROSÉ: pink | salmon | orange | copper

CLARITY:
clear | slight haze | cloudy

AROMA INTENSITY:
low | moderate | aromatic | powerful

DEVELOPMENT:
youthful | some age | aged

AROMAS:

DRY/SWEET:
bone dry | dry | off dry | medium sweet | sweet | very sweet

BODY:
very light | light | medium | medium-full | full-bodied | heavy

ACIDITY:
tart | crisp | fresh | smooth | flabby

TANNINS (IF PRESENT):
LEVEL: low | medium | high   TYPE: soft | round | dry | hard

BALANCE:
good | fair | unbalanced (excess: alcohol - acid - tannin - sugar)

FLAVOR INTENSITY:
low | moderate | flavorful | powerful

FLAVORS:

FINISH:
short (< 3 sec) | medium (4-5) | long (5-7) | v. long (>8 sec)

CONCLUSION:

STYLE:
traditional | in-between | modern

rating: ☆ ☆ ☆ ☆ ☆

FOOD: **FOOD PAIRING:**

MATCH: perfect | good | neutral | bad